KINGDOM
ENCOUNTERS

KINGDOM ENCOUNTERS

*Experiencing More of God
When Life Hurts*

TONY EVANS

Moody Publishers

CHICAGO

Edited by Kevin P. Emmert
Interior and cover design: Erik M. Peterson
Author photo: Anthony Amorteguy

Library of Congress Cataloging-in-Publication Data

Names: Evans, Tony, 1949- author.
Title: Kingdom encounters : experiencing more of God when life hurts / Tony Evans.
Description: Chicago : Moody Publishers, 2020. | Includes bibliographical references. | Summary: "What all Christians need is a kingdom encounter. In Kingdom Encounters, Tony Evans explores how the faithful characters of Scripture encountered God-and were forever changed. Join Dr. Evans as he explores how these moments bolster your faith, restore your hope, and make clear to you the face of God"-- Provided by publisher.
Identifiers: LCCN 2020020183 (print) | LCCN 2020020184 (ebook) | ISBN 9780802419255 | ISBN 9780802497901 (ebook)
Subjects: LCSH: God (Christianity)--Knowableness. | God (Christianity)--Attributes. | Experience (Religion) | Spirituality--Christianity.
Classification: LCC BT103 .E93 2020 (print) | LCC BT103 (ebook) | DDC 231.7--dc23
LC record available at https://lccn.loc.gov/2020020183
LC ebook record available at https://lccn.loc.gov/2020020184

Originally delivered by fleets of horse-drawn wagons, the affordable paperbacks from D. L. Moody's publishing house resourced the church and served everyday people. Now, after more than 125 years of publishing and ministry, Moody Publishers' mission remains the same—even if our delivery systems have changed a bit. For more information on other books (and resources) created from a biblical perspective, go to: www.moodypublishers.com or write to:

Moody Publishers
820 N. LaSalle Boulevard
Chicago, IL 60610

1 3 5 7 9 10 8 6 4 2

Printed in the United States of America

Contents

CHAPTER I

Encountering God's Person

Have you ever needed more than a Sunday morning service? Or a devotional on your smartphone? Have you ever felt like something was missing as you went through the motions of the Christian life? If that sounds familiar, you are a prime candidate for a kingdom encounter.

A kingdom encounter is when you discover how to connect with God by experience and not merely through information. The goal of a kingdom encounter is to give you and me a deeper, tangible experience of God's character and reality, and to take us to the next level of kingdom usefulness.

A person can attend church for years and never encounter God. A person can attend small groups every time they are offered and never experience the living and true Creator. God wants you to have more of Him than just theology on a shelf or information in your head. He wants to have an encounter with you that revolutionizes your life. Are you open to this?

Kingdom encounters most often come in the context of contradictions, challenges, and difficulties. They occur in times when you are facing conflict, when life seems off-kilter, or when things no longer make sense. It can feel conflicting at first. But what you need to realize—and what I hope you realize as you go through this book—is that when things are going left, you feel trapped and God seems absent, you are probably right where God wants you in order to experience a life-altering kingdom encounter.

My hope for you as you read through this book is that you will discover the delight and power of a divine encounter. That you will run smack dab into deity. That you will experience His presence at a level that leads to life transformation.

Far too many of us have a relationship with God that resembles the flicker of a candle more than the brilliance of a noonday sun. We go to church. We speak Christianese. We do our devotions. We post Scripture on social media. Yet we live with the pervading emptiness that results from a lack of encountering and experiencing the Most High God. As a result, we live lives of disappointment, pain, loss, regret, and hurt.

This reminds me of the story about a police officer who was called about a man planning to jump off a bridge to his death. When the policeman arrived at the scene, he began attempting to talk the man out of his suicide attempt. When he inquired why the man wanted to die, the man said that life was no longer worth living.

The policeman then gave the man an idea in order to buy time. He said, "Just give me ten minutes to explain why life is worth living. Then I'll give you ten minutes to tell me why it is not worth living. Then, if you still want to jump, I won't stop you." The man agreed.

The policeman began explaining eloquently about the meaning, significance, and importance of life. It was then the man's turn. He began to share how miserable things had been for him. A broken family, a failed career, bad health, deep debt, abuse, depression, and more. After he finished, the policeman reached out his hand to the man. The man grabbed it and they both jumped. Hopelessness has a way of metastasizing and spreading. Hopelessness can plague our hearts and minds so much that it makes itself present in more ways than we previously imagined possible.

I want that to change. I want more people to find hope. I want more people to heal from the hurt life has dealt them. I want more people to know the Lord in such a personal and experiential way that they can't help but be transformed and restored. I want you to encounter Him afresh, because once you do, you will never be the same again. Just like Moses, Elijah, Peter, Paul, Hannah, and the numerous others in Scripture whose encounters with God altered the trajectory of not only their lives but also the lives of generations to come.

One of the more well-known encounters in Scripture happened at a bush in the wild. Standing amidst the untamed wilderness on Mt. Horeb, Moses saw the living Lord. Pasturing his father-in-law's sheep on what most likely began as an ordinary day, Moses encountered the extraordinary. Standing alone, undoubtedly covered in dust and the wafting smell of the flock itself, he saw something (or Someone) that would forever rock his world.

Some backstory on Moses may help us appreciate how someone can potentially be positioned for a unique encounter. Moses wasn't always a shepherd. Moses hadn't always traveled the worn pathways of sheep on hillsides and mountains. No, Moses had grown up in the luxurious surroundings of a palace. Having been found by Pharaoh's daughter as he floated in a basket on the Nile River, placed there by his mother in an effort to secure his safety from the murderous plot of the Pharaoh to kill Israelite baby boys, Moses knew only comfort and provision. He knew power. He understood the Egyptian ways. He had not only glanced behind the curtain, but lived there as well.

Yet at the age of forty, Moses made a miscalculation. A misstep. He blew it. He decided to act independently of the one, true God and take matters into his own hands. Even though Moses had been raised in Egyptian culture and immersed in Egyptian thought, he knew enough to know the truth about his own people.

Even as he had grown in the midst of the Egyptian dynasty, God had still found a way to reach his heart. His biological mother had been called upon to serve as his nursemaid while he was still young; God's providential hand had orchestrated this for him. While his mother raised him and cared for him in those early years, she also told him the truth about God and His people.

By the time he had reached an age of ability and awareness, Moses no longer wanted to sit by and watch the injustices around him. He did not agree with how his people were being treated by the Egyptians. He wanted to secure their freedom. God had placed within his spirit an inkling of his true purpose

and calling, but rather than wait on God's ways and God's leading, Moses had decided to act on his own.

We read about this in Exodus 2:11–12:

> Now it came about in those days, when Moses had
> grown up, that he went out to his brethren and looked on
> their hard labors; and he saw an Egyptian beating a He-
> brew, one of his brethren. So, he looked this way and that,
> and when he saw there was no one around, he struck
> down the Egyptian and hid him in the sand.

The writer of Acts gives insight into Moses's thoughts at that
time. We read in Acts 7:25, "And he supposed that his brethren
understood that God was granting them deliverance through
him, but they did not understand." Moses believed that his purpose was to deliver his people, and his actions reflected it.

But as is the case with many of us, Moses had a sense of
destiny without the proper sense of divine timing. He tried to
force something that God had not yet unveiled. He used human
effort, opinion, logic, and strategy to attempt to accomplish a
divinely-appointed kingdom goal.

The goal was great: deliver God's people. His strategy and
timing, however, were off. As I said earlier, he blew it.

When Moses chose to act independently of God and depend
instead on his own expertise and self-sufficiency to accomplish
the plan of God for delivering His people, he inadvertently ushered in his own move from the palace to the pasture. We read
what happened next in Exodus 2:13–14:

He went out the next day, and behold, two Hebrews were fighting with each other; and he said to the offender, "Why are you striking your companion?" But he said, "Who made you a prince or a judge over us? Are you intending to kill me as you killed the Egyptian?" Then Moses was afraid and said, "Surely the matter has become known."

Moses's murder was discovered, and he had to run for his life. Moses ended up moving from the White House to the outhouse and spent the next forty years of his life in exile, herding dumb sheep on the backside of a desert.

When we find Moses in Exodus 3, we also find a forty-year gap between his murder and his encounter with God. Forty years span the divide between his failure and the divine revelation of his future. During those forty years, Moses led sheep in the wilderness. He was no longer in the spotlight. He was no longer "the man." He was no longer a high-profile celebrity in a culture of idol-worshiping and excess.

Rather, he was an outcast. A man in hiding. A man seeking to live as far away from Egypt as possible because what he had done wrong came with a high price tag tied to it. Moses had succumbed to a life of survival. He was just getting by. It is possible that even his dream of one day being used by God had dissipated into the heat of the sun-scorched land he now wandered.

Before we go any further in Moses's story, I want to ask you about your own. I want to ask you if you have ever led sheep or if you are leading them now. By that, I simply mean to ask if your life is not working out like you had hoped it would. It could be that something happened years ago that took you off course from your hopes. It could be that you are still struggling from a poor choice made early in your life. Did your dreams ever dissipate in the heat of disappointments, leaving you to wander around aimlessly, feeling trapped in a meaningless life with sheep?

Moses's early narrative isn't unique to him. Many people can identify with it. While it may not have been something as extreme as murder, poor choices in a person's life can still send them scrambling to regain what had once been lost. Or even send them into a wilderness just to wander on their own. God has given each of us free will. We are able to make our own choices. What we often forget is that those choices come with consequences that are most often outside of our control.

If you are one of the many who wishes they could go back and redo it, avoid it, or overcome it, Moses's story has you in mind. If you are just trying to make it, doing the best you can while leading sheep, and life seems to be dragging on, one endless day after another, Moses's encounter with God holds hope for you. After all, Moses shepherded sheep for forty years. From the time of his infraction to the time of his encounter, he spent countless days counting sheep.

So as we begin our exploration of encounters with God, I want to start by giving you some good news, particularly for those of you who are reading this and find yourselves in a dry place. If your life has become dull and dreary as you carry out your day-to-day routine, the good news of Moses is great news for you. Because as you have watched the calendar simply go by or have heard the tick-tock of the clock year after year, decade after decade, God has been watching you. God has not forgotten about you. God has a plan for you. If you are still here, that means there is still hope for a fresh encounter with God.

God does some of His best work in the dark, even when we don't think He is doing anything at all. He does some of His best maneuvering and intersecting in those gaps when we feel as if He isn't even near. Your purpose and your destiny aren't about only you. While you may be wandering in the wilderness, God is working out the details of His plan in those He will one day connect you to. We will see this play out in the story of Moses as well as in the stories of others who have encountered God.

THE VICINITY

As we look at Moses's encounter, let us begin by taking a look at where he is. According Exodus 3:1, he is on the "the west side of the wilderness and came to Horeb, the mountain of God." To clarify, the mountain of God, or Horeb, is Mt. Sinai. This is also the mountain where God's presence would be manifested in a miraculous way to Moses not long after this first experience, where God would give Moses the Ten Commandments.

While it goes by many names, this place is historically known as the mountain of God. This tells us that Moses experiences an encounter with God because he is first and foremost in God's vicinity.

A lot of people want an experience with God but do not want to hang out where God is located. They choose to place themselves outside of His vicinity. But if you want an experience with God, the first lesson to learn is that you have to hang out where He is. The pursuit of God includes the willingness and intention to go into God's presence. As long as you insist on a long-distance relationship with God, that is precisely the relationship you will have. Anyone who chooses not to pursue the proximity and vicinity of God will live absent of divinely ordained kingdom encounters.

Moses did not get his encounter with God until he reached the mountain of God. While there, we read in Exodus 3:2 that the angel of the Lord appeared to him. It says,

> The angel of the LORD appeared to him in a blazing fire from the midst of a bush; and he looked, and behold, the bush was burning with fire, yet the bush was not consumed.

We know that the angel of the Lord is equated with God in this verse because later in verse 4, it tells us that "God" spoke to Moses from the midst of the bush. Whenever the angel of the Lord is equated with God in the Old Testament, it is the manifestation of the second person of the Trinity (Jesus Christ), acting as the spokesperson for the Father since He is the incarnate Word of God (see John 1:1, 14).

Before we get to what God said, let us take a look at what God did. After all, Moses had probably seen a number of burning bushes in his day. He shepherded sheep in the dry atmosphere of a wilderness. Brush fires happened all the time. But this particular fire was unusual because this particular fire burned without consuming the bush.

The fire itself was not what caught Moses's attention. He could have easily removed his attention and guided his sheep elsewhere. However, this fire grabbed his focus for another reason altogether. This fire wasn't doing what normal fires do, which is to consume that which it is burning.

What Moses saw was a contradiction. He became an eyewitness to the wonder of God's power. And one of the ways you can know you are on the precipice of an encounter with God is when He presents you with a contradictory situation. Throughout the Bible, you will see contradictions occurring when God shows up. We can identify a pattern of things not operating according to the normal flow. If a bush is on fire, for example, it is supposed be burning up. Yet if there is a bush on fire and the wood is staying the same, and the leaves are staying the same, and nothing is being consumed, that is not normal. That is not how things roll on earth. That ought to get your attention. Similarly, in your own life, when you experience something outside of normative patterns for life, open your eyes. When you see things that don't make sense, pay attention. If stuff just doesn't add up, focus in. Because you may be on the verge of a divine kingdom encounter.

When or if that happens, do what Moses did. When Moses saw the burning bush, it stopped him in his tracks. We read in Exodus 3:3, "So Moses said, 'I must turn aside now and see this marvelous sight, why the bush is not burned up.'" Moses didn't skip it. He didn't gloss over it. He didn't rationalize it. Rather, he investigated it. He turned toward the anomaly in order to understand what was going on.

Many of us have missed an encounter with God because we have ignored the contradictions He has placed before us. We have ignored the thing that didn't add up, or the situation that didn't make sense. We have brushed it aside either out of fear or doubt. We have shrugged it off. But in doing so, we have also distanced ourselves from an experience God desired us to have with Him.

Moses turned aside to examine the contradiction. He sought clarity in the confusion. As he did, he heard God call him. Verse 4 says, "When the LORD saw that he turned aside to look, God called to him from the midst of the bush and said, 'Moses, Moses!' And he said, 'Here I am.'"

Notice when God called Moses. It wasn't until after Moses had responded to the contradiction. "When the LORD saw . . . God called to him."

In Matthew 13:12, we find the principle that when we respond to God and what He has done, He will then give more. It's a causation-based principle. We read, "For whoever has, to him more shall be given, and he will have an abundance." It's another way of warning us that when God shows up in our lives, we ought not to ignore it. We need to respond to what He reveals because in doing so, He will give more. God is not about to waste His ways or His glory on those who do not pick up on it, care to know, or use it to bring Him more glory.

When God gives you a contradiction, it is not to be ignored or dismissed. It is to be investigated. You are to intentionally seek a clearer understanding of what has occurred by seeking God Himself. God didn't do anything directly related to Moses until after He saw what Moses did.

God is not interested in what you are saying. He is interested in what you do. Talk is cheap. It's easy enough to say what you are going to do. It's easy enough to say you are going to pray, fast, or seek God. It's easy to talk a good spiritual game. But God responds to what you *do*. Just like He did with Moses.

When God saw Moses turn aside, He called to him from the midst of the bush. He spoke to him personally. When God speaks outside of the context of Scripture, it is called a *rhema* word. These are the times when you know that the Holy Spirit is speaking to you as well. It could be something that happens in a church service you are attending. Or maybe during a sermon you are listening to on your radio or smartphone. It could occur as you are praying or reading Scripture. It is in those times when you simply know that God is speaking to you personally, but always consistently with His written Word.

Even though no one else may be there, and no one else may understand, God still speaks to us through rhema words today. He speaks through circumstances and signs, which come to you as an utterance with your name written all over it. My role as a pastor allows me the unique opportunity to hear about these rhema words from a variety of people. Whenever I deliver a sermon, it is a general message intended for everyone who hears it. And yet, without fail, different people will tell me later how God spoke directly to them through the message.

This reminds me of the time when I was at a conference where former President George W. Bush was speaking. He gave a general presidential message to the entire audience, but in the midst of his presentation, he looked my way and called me out by name. When you are in God's presence, He knows how to call your name even in the midst of a crowd.

The Holy Spirit takes spiritual truths and applies them to the various situations of life we experience. He speaks. Unfortunately, far too many people miss out on hearing Him speak because they either fail to turn aside and seek to understand the unusual occurrences life produces, or they don't even notice them. But for those who do notice, God has a word for you. The question is: Do you hear it? When God grabs your undivided attention because He wants to show up in your presence, are you open enough to hearing what He has to say?

My best advice to you is that if you are in a wilderness, look for God to show up in a way that you can't explain. His ways are not your ways; His thoughts are not your thoughts (Isa. 55:8–9). God is not like you or me. If God were living in the era of soul music, His favorite song would be, "Didn't I (Blow Your Mind This Time)?" Didn't I show up in a way that you couldn't explain? That's what God does. Look for it. Then draw near to Him at your own Mt. Horeb.

Moses heard His voice. As a result, Moses got to experience what is now known and called the "shekinah glory" of God. This is the specific glory God reveals when He manifests Himself. Keep in mind that God exists even when we don't see His glory, just as the sun still exists even on an overcast day. But to see His glory is to experience His existence. When you walk outside, the air is everywhere. Yet when the wind starts blowing, you experience the moving air, and you see its impact. The air exists whether or not it is moving. But when it moves, the air becomes an experience.

God is everywhere. He is omnipresent. He exists everywhere at the same time, beyond all time. But God's shekinah glory is what you and I experience when we encounter His movement in the midst of our lives. That's when we get to hear Him speak, like Moses did. Friend, if you are desiring a kingdom encounter with the living God as you wander in your personal wilderness, you must be in His presence. You must respond to those things around you that don't make sense. When you do, you will position yourself to hear from Him directly. As you place your heart and mind in His presence through prayer and the Word, you are placing yourself on the mountain of God. You are making yourself available to God for an encounter with Him.

God met Moses on the mountain. He called his name. To which Moses replied, "Here I am" (Ex. 3:4). God then gave Moses some instructions. He told him not to come nearer to the bush. He also told him to take off his sandals because the place on which he stood was holy (v. 5). Now, if you pass over that information, you may miss something vital to your spiritual understanding and growth. Let's look at it again:

> God is speaking from the bush.
> Moses is standing on the ground.
> Moses is told not to come closer to the bush.
> Moses is in God's territory now, which extends beyond
>   the direct location of the bush itself.
> Moses realizes he is standing on holy ground.
> Moses must remove his shoes.

The holy ground on which Moses stood wasn't the bush itself.

It was the ground surrounding the bush. It included the vicinity. God insisted Moses take off his shoes because the location was holy. Moses's shoes were dirty, as all shoes are. Many people post notices at the door to their homes to politely ask people to remove their shoes. This is because shoes track in the dirt from outside.

Dirt and holiness do not mix. Let me make something clear as we study this process of kingdom encounters: You cannot have an encounter with God if you are unwilling to deal with your personal sin. If you are unwilling to acknowledge and repent of your sin, you can't even get close to the bush. God is holy. His presence is holy. To enter into His presence, you have to be willing to take off your shoes and remove the dirt you have accumulated along life's path.

Holy means "to be separate." It refers to someone or something that is sacredly separate. Thus, to enter into God's holy presence, we have to separate ourselves from the sin that stains us. The only plan given for that separation is called confession and repentance. First John 1:9 puts it this way, "If we confess our sins, He is faithful and righteous to forgive us our sins and to cleanse us from all unrighteousness."

Repentance is the internal decision and determination to turn away from sin and simultaneously turn toward God in reverence, gratitude, and awe. The writer of Acts tells us that repentance is tied to entering into an encounter with God. It says in Acts 3:19, "Therefore repent and return, so that your sins may be wiped away, in order that times of refreshing may come from the presence of the Lord."

Moses was instructed to remove his shoes because he stood on holy ground. He had to sever himself from the dirt that polluted him, symbolically, in God's presence. Likewise, we as believers must come to God with a spirit of repentance, forsaking our sin, and receiving His cleansing forgiveness. David modeled the need for and heart of repentance in his psalm of repentance (Ps. 51). His prayer is instructive as to how we are to enter into God's presence. Let's look at a portion of it:

> Hide Your face from my sins
> And blot out all my iniquities.
>
> Create in me a clean heart, O God,
> And renew a steadfast spirit within me.
> Do not cast me away from Your presence
> And do not take Your Holy Spirit from me.
> Restore to me the joy of Your salvation
> And sustain me with a willing spirit.
> Then I will teach transgressors Your ways,
> And sinners will be converted to You.
>
> Deliver me from bloodguiltiness, O God, the God of my
>   salvation;
> Then my tongue will joyfully sing of Your righteousness.
> O Lord, open my lips,
> That my mouth may declare Your praise.
> For You do not delight in sacrifice, otherwise I would give
>   it;
> You are not pleased with burnt offering.

> The sacrifices of God are a broken spirit;
> A broken and a contrite heart, O God, You will not
> despise. (vv. 9–17)

God is not asking that we sacrifice something for His for-giveness. That sacrifice was made perfectly for us through the sinless life, death, and resurrection of Jesus Christ. What we are instructed to do, as we see in this psalm, is to come to God in a broken spirit with a contrite heart to ask for His forgiveness. When that is done, forgiveness is given, and we can rest assured in the complete absolution through Jesus Christ. Romans 8:1 offers this hope, "Therefore there is now no condemnation for those who are in Christ Jesus."

Because Moses willingly removed his shoes—obeying God's commands—he entered into a greater encounter with the living God. Removing his shoes also demonstrated humility in God's presence since Moses's feet were now directly on the dirt from which he was created. Moses was a creature in the presence of his Creator. But please notice what God used in order to speak to Moses. Even though it was a highly contradictory situation, God used an ordinary object. The bush was already there. It was simply an ordinary bush that had been invaded by God's super-natural presence that resulted in an extraordinary encounter.

I don't know how God is going to meet you, but I do know that any old bush will do. God can use the most ordinary thing and set fire to it in order to create the most ingenious contradic-tion that allows a greater manifestation of His power and glory. But let me remind you, if this is going to happen to you, you cannot be a flame-resistant Christian.

People put on flame-resistant suits when they work in close proximity to flames so that they won't catch fire. Some of us believers will never burn with the brilliance of the Holy Spirit's power made manifest in and through us because we wear evangelical flame-resistant suits. We really don't want to get close to the fire of God's presence. We don't want God to rub off on us like that. So, to protect ourselves from that which we cannot explain or rationalize, we put on our intellectual or emotional flame-resistant attire, and we come to church, leaving on our flame-resistant shoes. All the while, we wonder why we don't catch fire for the Lord.

God's miraculous manifestations are for those who have the faith to enter into His presence and the humility to surrender to His instructions.

Once Moses responded to God and took off his shoes, God revealed to him who He was. We read this in Exodus 3:6–7 where it says,

> "I am the God of your father, the God of Abraham, the God of Isaac, and the God of Jacob." Then Moses hid his face, for he was afraid to look at God.
>
> The LORD said, "I have surely seen the affliction of My people who are in Egypt and have given heed to their cry because of their taskmasters, for I am aware of their sufferings."

God makes Himself known to Moses by first identifying who He is: the God of his father, the God of Abraham, the God of Isaac, and the God of Jacob. He reminds Moses of His history before He tells Moses of what is to come. Not only that, He also lets Moses know that He has seen the affliction of the Israelites in Egypt, and He is aware of the same atrocities that plagued Moses's heart some forty years earlier.

Remember that this whole thing started years ago. Moses thought he knew what he was supposed to do, to be used by God to deliver the people. He knew God had a handle on his life. He just hadn't gone about it God's way. The calling and purpose were clear. The path just got distorted because Moses had too much Egypt in him at that time, to the degree that he sought to bring about the resolution through his own methods and means.

But, by introducing Himself to Moses in this way, God let Moses know that He had not forgotten the covenantal promises He made to Moses's ancestors or what He had planned to do through Moses. God had not forgotten what He had planned to do for His people either to fulfill those promises.

It is important to point out here that God's delays are often tied to our development. Because Moses would one day be called upon to lead the lost sheep of the house of Israel, God gave him forty years of experience leading sheep through a wilderness until his self-confidence was ready to be shifted to God-confidence.

God's delays are also tied to Him creating a scenario to be most ideal for His purpose. While God was developing Moses, He was also making a spiritual link between the condition of the Israelites with Moses's own maturity. Moses thought he was ready to deliver Israel forty years earlier. He had the education, wealth, eloquence, power, and raw materials to do it. But what he didn't have was a dependence on God evidenced by spiritual maturity and humility. God is always after developing our spiritual maturity before bringing us into our destiny. He wants to connect our character with our calling.

God also prepares other parts of the purpose while He is preparing the person to live it out. The Israelites didn't know what God was doing to solve their problem as they cried out to Him to deliver them from the Egyptians. They definitely weren't daydreaming about a hero-shepherd-man from Midian. But God was getting ready to make a divine encounter where He was arranging both situations to meet at the right time.

These kingdom encounters are God-ordained points of connection that only He knows beforehand. We don't know what, where, or how God is going to arrange kingdom encounters. All we can do is proceed with our development, trusting God to bring us to the point where we are ready for that connection to take place at the proper time.

There may be something God put on your heart to do years ago, but it has yet to be fulfilled. I don't know how long you may have been struggling as you wait on God. Or perhaps you have gotten to the point where you have given up hope that He will even do anything at all. But I want to encourage you to keep your eyes open for the living Lord. God hasn't forgotten you. He knows where you are. He knows how you got there. He knows how long you have been there. And like He did with Moses, He can call your name for you to carry out the plan He's placed on your life, even if you have gotten off the timetable you had once envisioned for your life.

The first half of a football game is never the whole story for how things will wind up. Many a team that was losing in the first half winds up winning the game in the end. Much of this shift comes because of their meeting with the coach at half-time when adjustments are made. So if your story up to this point is one of loss, defeat, regret, and disappointment, then meet with God at your burning bush. Or, if necessary, ask Him to give you one. He can reverse the things that make it appear that your life is over. He can move you from a regular existence to a premium, super-unleaded one and bring you to a victorious life as you discover and fulfill your kingdom destiny.

CHAPTER 2

Encountering God's Power

After church one day, a mother asked her son, "What did your Sunday school teacher teach you today in Sunday school?"

He answered, "Well, Mama, the Sunday school teacher taught us about Israel crossing the Red Sea."

So she asked, "What did the teacher say about Israel crossing the Red Sea?"

To which her son replied, "Well, it was like this—Israel built a bridge over the Red Sea. They got in busses and crossed over the bridge. Then when the Egyptians came after them, God sent some F-16 fighters and dropped bombs on them so that they were destroyed."

The mother stood there with a stunned look on her face. "Come on, now! Your teacher couldn't have explained Israel crossing the Red Sea like that!"

Her son laughed and said, "Well, if you had heard what she said, you wouldn't have believed it either!"

The little boy made up that story because the reality is, the way the Israelites really did cross the Red Sea is unfathomable to our human minds. God's ways are so much higher than our ways, and even so much higher and broader than our understanding (Isa. 55:8–9). Faith plays such a critical role in our relationship with God because our finite minds cannot comprehend the full extent of His power.

Sometimes God's power shows up directly like in the ability to speak from a burning bush that does not burn up. Other times His power appears responsively as in the time the Centurion asked Jesus to heal his servant just by saying the word (Luke 7:1–10). Yet there are also those times, and they happen frequently throughout Scripture, where we see the manifestation of God's power in the context of a dilemma. A dilemma is a situation where there is no clear answer. No matter where you look or how many solutions you run through your own mind, confusion remains the overriding thought.

Dilemmas have a lot of nicknames. Some people call a dilemma being in a jam. Other people call it a catch-22. Others say they are in a pit. You may have heard the phrase "up a creek without a paddle." That phrase describes a dilemma. More phrases include:

Backed into a corner.
Being up a tree.
Faced with a dead-end situation.
Having your back up against a wall.

Between a rock and hard place.

Stuck in a trickbag.

Dilemmas are simply those situations we call "no-win scenarios." Any direction that you choose is a lose-lose. There's no way out, up, or over. You're stuck.

Stuck is exactly how the Israelites found themselves as they made their way from slavery to freedom. You could say they had been backed into a corner. But it would be more appropriate to say they had been backed up against a bank. The bank of the Red Sea was as far as they could go as the Egyptian army chased after them.

The crossing of the Red Sea is one of the most celebrated stories in all Scripture. It is referenced time and again, including in the New Testament. Hebrews 11:29 says, "By faith they passed through the Red Sea as though they were passing through dry land; and the Egyptians, when they attempted it, were drowned." This is no small occurrence. What happened at the Red Sea has lessons within lessons within lessons for us. But for the purposes of this book and this chapter, I want us to start by examining the context.

GOD'S PROVIDENCE

Israel had their kingdom encounter with God in the context of what looked like an unsolvable dilemma.

The Israelites were undoubtedly feeling strong, hopeful, and uplifted after seeing the strong hand of God deliver plague after plague on the Egyptians in order to secure their freedom. Songs had to have been sung as they they traveled in their caravan out of bondage. They were excited. They were looking forward to new beginnings. They had been told of the Promised Land, which held all that was needed for them to form their own nation. They felt secure in the purpose of God and His power to fulfill that purpose for them. Where God was taking them must have looked rosy.

But where they first wound up didn't look too rosy at all. There they stood, with the sound of the hooves of the Egyptian horses closing in, facing a great body of water they could not pass through on their own. The question that must have come to many of them, if not most, is why were they there in the first place? They could have gone a different route and made their journey a lot quicker. No doubt they questioned the wisdom of their leader who had taken them on not only a longer path, but now it seemed as if it were at a dead end—literally.

But Moses had not made this decision to go this way. God had. We see this in Exodus 13:17–18:

> Now when Pharaoh had let the people go, God did not lead them by the way of the land of the Philistines, even though it was near; for God said, "The people might change their minds when they see war, and return to Egypt." Hence God led the people around by the way of the wilderness to the Red Sea; and the sons of Israel went up in martial array from the land of Egypt.

The Israelites' dilemma didn't take place as an accident. God wasn't in heaven looking down, saying, "Oops, I should have told them to go the other way!" No, the Israelite's seemingly no-win situation happened on purpose. God's providential hand led them there. They ran into the Red Sea because they were in the will of God. They faced their challenge out of a decision to be obedient. God Himself led them. Not only did He lead them to the Sea, but the Scripture we just looked at tells us that He led them the long way around on their journey. He did not take them on a straight path.

Perhaps you feel like He has done something similar with you. I know I have at times. There are situations when it seems like God takes a person from A to F and then back to C, only to later wind up at X and then next on to T. It can create feelings of frustration, causing questions as to why God didn't just take a straight-line approach.

In times of doubt that arise like these, you must remember that God always has a purpose in what He does. God took the Israelites on the long route on purpose. He took them to the edge of the Red Sea on purpose. In fact, He led them straight into the corner Himself. In Exodus 13:21–22, we read about Him leading them:

> The LORD was going before them in a pillar of cloud by
> day to lead them on the way, and in a pillar of fire by
> night to give them light, that they might travel by day and
> by night. He did not take away the pillar of cloud by day,
> nor the pillar of fire by night, from before the people.

God had the Israelites right where He wanted them. He wanted them there so badly that He didn't even allow for the opportunity for them to get lost. During the day, He led them by a pillar of cloud. At night, He led them by a pillar of fire. This was His plan. And His plan had a very important purpose.

So critical was this purpose that God told Moses to have the people camp by the sea. He knew Pharaoh would see what they were doing, assume they were trapped, and chase after them. We read about this as the story progresses in Exodus 14:1–4. It says,

> Now the LORD spoke to Moses, saying, "Tell the sons of Israel to turn back and camp before Pi-hahiroth, be-tween Migdol and the sea; you shall camp in front of Baal-zephon, opposite it, by the sea. For Pharaoh will say of the sons of Israel, 'They are wandering aimlessly in the land; the wilderness has shut them in.' Thus, I will harden Pharaoh's heart, and he will chase after them; and I will be honored through Pharaoh and all his army, and the Egyptians will know that I am the LORD." And they did so.

It was God's plan for Pharaoh to see what the Israelites were doing and think that they had walked straight into a cul-de-sac of sorts. That way Pharoah would believe they were trapped and thus summon the courage to send a large fleet of his army after them, which is exactly what he did. At the time, this plan couldn't have made any amount of sense to the Israelites as they stared at the Red Sea blocking their advance. Similarly, I'm sure God's plans don't always make sense to us either. Many of us fig-ure that God would never lead us into a trap and begin to doubt God when there seems to be no way out. But those are the times when the history and truth of the Bible ought to remind us that we should trust Him the most.

Traps are often intentional. Because there's one overarching reality that exists in every trap scenario—you can't get out of it on your own. Sometimes God lets you hit rock bottom so that you will see that He is the Rock at the bottom. When you don't see an exit, He is the exit. And the reason why He wants you and I to encounter Him at this level is to move us into a new spiritual experience with Him. God will regularly reveal Himself in the midst of a contradiction and conflict in order to awaken our hearts and minds to His great power.

Unfortunately, far too many of us are like the schoolchild whom I used as an illustration to open this chapter. We don't take the historicity of the Bible literally. We toss it away as fable or story, thinking those things surely couldn't have happened that way. Or others of us believe it only for that period of time. There are those who think that the miracles and kingdom encounters of the Old Testament were for a season and that God doesn't work that way anymore. As a result, we lack the faith necessary to follow obediently the pillar of cloud by day and pillar of fire by night leading the way.

Yet the book of Romans tells us that the reason we were given these historical recordings was precisely so that we would apply their spiritual principles in our lives today. They were given to us in order to give us hope. Romans 15:4 says, "For whatever was written in earlier times was written for our instruction, so that through perseverance and the encouragement of the Scriptures we might have hope."

The story of the Red Sea doesn't exist solely for the purposes of the Israelites. The story of the Red Sea, and what it means, is also for us. It has been placed there by God, so that in hearing and believing it, we will have hope for our trap scenarios in life. It has been passed down to us through the canonization of Scripture to give each of us the perspective and insight we need in those times when we don't see an exit. It was written for our instruction.

Even the part that speaks of God hardening Pharaoh's heart, because he insisted on hardening his own heart (Ex. 8:32), was written for our instruction. God Himself chose for that to happen. He caused it to happen. He encouraged the chase when the Israelites felt trapped because it was in the midst of the chase they would discover His power to deliver.

Does it ever seem when you are praying for a change in a situation that the situation just gets worse? Maybe the boss gets meaner or the spouse becomes more distant. Or it could be that the circumstances become even more negative than they were before you prayed. So you throw your hands up and wonder why you bothered to pray at all. It's okay to admit this has happened to you. I'm sure the Israelites wondered why they were pressed up against a dead end like they were, only to have it get worse with the Egyptians chasing after them. It could almost seem like God's involvement was making things worse.

Which is exactly what He did. He took the anger of Pharaoh and made him more angry. He took the hatred of Pharaoh and notched it up a bit. He allowed Pharaoh's hardened heart to develop even greater levels of resentment toward the Israelites so that Pharoah, in his free will, would choose to take a large army and chase after them into what appeared (to the Egyptians at least) a no-lose scenario.

Friend, when God is getting ready to give you a new experience with His power, He will regularly allow you to run out of options without Him. When He is ready to let you see Him in a way you've never seen Him before, expect that you will be in a situation that you cannot handle alone so that He is your only option.

Now, if you don't know this spiritual truth or you have a false view of God and the devil that boxes every negative occurrence into the devil's domain, you will not be positioned to see God's deliverance in those times when He wants to deliver you. Be careful to never ascribe to the devil what may actually be the hand of God. The Israelites are smack-dab in the will of God. And they are stuck. As a result, and understandably, they were also afraid. We read about this in Exodus 14:10: "As Pharaoh drew near, the sons of Israel looked, and behold, the Egyptians were marching after them, and they became very frightened; so the sons of Israel cried out to the LORD."

In their fear, the Israelites cried out to the Lord. They had done that during their captivity, and God had come to their defense. It makes sense that they would do it again here. The problem came, though, when they chose to do more than cry out to God. Lacking faith, the Israelites resorted to blame and complaining. Verses 11–12 say,

> Then they said to Moses, "Is it because there were no graves in Egypt that you have taken us away to die in

the wilderness? Why have you dealt with us in this
way, bringing us out of Egypt? Is this not the word that we
spoke to you in Egypt, saying, 'Leave us alone that we may
serve the Egyptians'? For it would have been better for us
to serve the Egyptians than to die in the wilderness."

By that time, the Israelites were questioning their own freedom. They chose to call on God while simultaneously blaming
Moses. Their desperation had grown so deep that they resorted
to rhetoric about their own deaths. Mocking Moses's leadership,
they asked him if there were no graves in Egypt, accusing him of
taking them into the wilderness to die. Moses must have thought
about the time forty years earlier when he had attempted to deliver the Israelites through his own method—the wrong method
of murder—and suffered the Israelites' wrath. I wonder if Moses
questioned whether he had heard from God rightly on this
method as well. I wonder if he feared the fear and hatred now
being directed at him. I wonder if he doubted himself.

We don't know exactly what Moses was thinking, although
we get a glimpse in a later verse. We know how he responded.
He responded with confidence. He responded with faith. He
responded as a man who had already experienced a kingdom
encounter that had increased his own ability to take God at His
word. Moses tapped into the history of his relationship with
God and told the Israelites to (in my Tony Evans's translation)
"shut up." It is written for us in Scripture like this:

"Do not fear! Stand by and see the salvation of
the LORD which He will accomplish for you today; for the

Egyptians whom you have seen today, you will never see
them again forever. The LORD will fight for you while you
keep silent." (vv. 13–14)

Let me repeat that last part: "The LORD will fight for you
while you keep silent." The truth of this verse can be worded in
other ways as well, while still maintaining its validity. You could
say, "He won't fight for you while you are talking." Or even, "He
won't fight for you while you are whining." Both of these statements paint the same picture as what we are given in Moses's
reply to the Israelites.

Rather than trust the same God who had just miraculously
rained frogs from heaven, turned water into blood, caused the
sky to be dark during the day, and a number of other powerful
displays, the Israelites ran their mouths. In doing so, they kept
their focus on humanity rather than divinity. They lost sight of
the divine action that had directed them there in the first place.
Moses was a more mature man than I would have been in the
same situation because I might have worded it differently: "God
will not fight for you until you shut up!"

OUR ONLY SOLUTION

The spiritual truths that existed for the Israelites in this scenario
remain true for us today. As long as you or I have diarrhea of
the mouth, we will be limiting our ability to witness God's divine power. As long as complaining trumps trusting, we are
blocking the very kingdom encounter we need most. Followers
of Christ must get out of the habit of complaining or blaming

when things go wrong. We must learn how to shut up and let God do His thing.

God *will* fight for you while you keep silent. God will deliver you while you focus on Him. God will reveal Himself to you while you refrain from blaming circumstances, people, or the powers that be. He did it for the Israelites, and He will do it for you—if you will obey His commands in a spirit of surrender, hope, and gratitude.

Now, don't get me wrong. I'm not saying this is easy. As I mentioned earlier, we do get a small glimpse into what Moses was thinking at this time. And even though he was a man who had experienced God in powerful and mighty ways, we can discern from the passage that he was also afraid. Verses 15–16 tell us that God answered him with a rebuke of sorts:

> Then the LORD said to Moses, "Why are you crying out to Me? Tell the sons of Israel to go forward. As for you, lift up your staff and stretch out your hand over the sea and divide it, and the sons of Israel shall go through the midst of the sea on dry land."

Please notice that God started off by asking Moses why he was crying out to Him. Now, the problem with that verse is that nothing is stated previously about Moses crying out to Him. What we read in the passage is that the people cried out to God. But somewhere between the people crying out and Moses answering the people, he himself had to have cried out to God. As a pastor, I can understand this. Because when a pastor is in the pulpit, he preaches from the Word of God. He knows the answers. He gives the answers from the Bible. When you're in the pulpit, it's easy to encourage others to remember that God is their rock, their sword, their shield—He's the wheel in the middle of the wheel! It's not hard to say those things! After all, God is good—all the time. He *is* the balm of Gilead, the bright and morning star! Reminding people of these truths comes naturally to a lot of preachers grounded in God's Word.

But preachers are human. We face our struggles. We have our doubts. We get backed into our own corners. And when we do, we sometimes get scared ourselves. That being so, I can easily picture Moses telling the Israelites to hush their fuss and trust God while simultaneously turning to God internally and crying out, "Help us! What are You going to do? We're stuck!" Even leaders sometimes have their faith challenged about the very things they are preaching on. Which is why it's so critical for spiritual leaders to stay in close communication with God.

After all, Moses just told the Israelites to "stand by." This could be translated as "hold still." A statement like that makes perfect sense in light of the reality that there was really nowhere for them to go anyhow. Yet when Moses secretly cried out to God, God told him to tell the Israelites to "go forward." It's good that Moses cried out to God.

The spiritual principle is this: When God puts you in a dilemma and there is nothing you can or should do, you do nothing. You "stand by." But while you are standing by, continue to seek Him. Continue to cry out to Him. Continue to ask Him for direction, even though you can't even fathom what kind of direction He might give. Because even though the Israelites were up against an uncrossable sea, God told them to go forward.

God's guidance will always require faith to follow. As we see in Hebrews 11:29, "By faith they passed through the Red Sea as though they were passing through dry land." Remember, faith is in your feet, not in your feelings. You may feel full of faith but have no faith because faith always shows up in what you do. If your feet aren't moving when God has given you an instruction to move, then you are faithless. In fact, a person can feel no faith at all but at the same time, be full of faith because their decisions are done in obedience to God's revealed will. Faith is never to be measured by your feelings. Faith is in your feet.

Faith must operate when fear is present. Faith does not automatically eradicate or remove fear; it overrides it. Fear immobilizes. Faith moves, even if a person is fearful. Until God sees faith, you don't see God. Hebrews 11:6 tells us that faith is God's love language, "And without faith it is impossible to please Him, for he who comes to God must believe that He is and that He is a rewarder of those who seek Him."

God rewards those who seek Him. God rewards faith. The reverse of both of those statements is true as well. You will see over and over again in Scripture that God withheld His involvement until the people did something. He waited until He saw what they did, as a result of their faith. See, a lot of us are waiting on God to move when God is actually waiting on us. We may talk a good faith-game. But if our feet haven't moved in response to His revealed will, we are all talk with no walk. Unless you operate on what God has told you to do, you are not pleasing God. Faith pleases God. Without faith, it is impossible to please Him.

God had told Moses two things when He gave him instructions on what to do with their backs up against the bank of the Red Sea. First, He said, "As for you, Moses, do this." And then He said, "As for Me, I will do this." He said, "Moses, first you need to act. You need to take that little stick that you've been using to lead sheep around with, and you need to hold that out because it is now sanctified."

In other words, God said He wasn't going to do His role until Moses first did his. He wanted Moses to step out in faith. Not only that, but He asked Moses to step out in faith with the very object he had spent forty years of development with in the wilderness. He wanted Moses to use the staff that he led his sheep with for all of those years.

A lot of what God asks us to do in our personal lives is tied to the very things we learn from this story of Moses. It is often tied to what we used and developed during our wilderness times. Those times were not wasted. Those times when you felt like nothing was going on, everything was going on. God was preparing you for your destiny.

Keep in mind, the move God asks us to do isn't typically all that huge. He doesn't call us to swoop through the sky like Superman. All God asked him to do was to hold out his stick. That's not that huge of a move. If Moses would just hold out his stick, then God said He'd handle the rest. He'd do all the big stuff. He'd open the Red Sea, harden Pharaoh's heart, make him go in after them, and close the Red Sea up again.

But to reveal the faith within us, God often asks us to do our little thing first. Hold out our sticks. Take that step. Make the move. Have the conversation. Quit the job to stay at home. Accept the job that He has shown. Stop the habit. Curb the tongue. Repent in private. Go to church. Give. Whatever it is that He is revealing to you, God will often wait to do His big thing until you do what He has asked you to do.

He does this because He wants us to see and encounter Him in a way we've never seen and encountered Him before. He wants us to see the connection between our act of faith and His hand of deliverance. He wants to be more than just a cosmic Santa Claus with a pocketful of miracles to throw down. God wants a relationship with you. He wants you to see Him up close and personal.

So to accomplish this, He puts you in a situation where He is your only solution. Where it can't be fixed if He doesn't fix it. Where it can't be reversed if He doesn't reverse it. Where it can't be solved if He doesn't solve it. Because, He says, I've let you use all of the natural options available to you, and you are still stuck. Well then, you are stuck with a purpose.

But before He does anything at all, He often asks us to hold out our stick.

Yes, you might feel silly holding out a small stick over a huge body of water that doesn't seem to be going anywhere. But if you'll do it when He asks you to do it, He'll do everything that He has promised. Just like He did for the Israelites when He led them through a body of water on dry land.

When the Israelites got to the other side of the Red Sea, and they saw how God had closed the waters on top of the Egyptian horses and their riders, they broke into song. Their complaints changed to a chorus because now they had seen God firsthand. They had a kingdom encounter.

This kingdom encounter produced what God desired it to produce in them. It produced an awe of Him, His power, and His glory. We read about this in the close of Exodus 14:

> Thus the LORD saved Israel that day from the hand of the Egyptians, and Israel saw the Egyptians dead on the sea-shore. When Israel saw the great power which the LORD had used against the Egyptians, the people feared the LORD, and they believed in the LORD and in His servant Moses. (vv. 30–31)

They feared and believed in the Lord. Why does God put you in a dilemma when you are in the middle of His will? So that you can encounter Him at a whole new level, thus increasing both your fear of Him (reverence) and your belief in Him (faith).

If you are tired of other people's testimonies while not having your own, seek God in those circumstances that you can't seem to solve. Don't complain. Don't blame. Don't look for a way to maneuver yourself out. Rather, cry out to God. Then, when He tells you what to do, do it. When the Israelites encountered the power of the Lord, they encountered God Himself.

God was trying to deliver the Israelites from something more than just their bondage. He was trying to deliver them from their past. You saw how quickly they wanted to run back to Egypt when things got hard. Egypt was familiar. It may have been bondage, but it rarely required faith. But God knew that the Promised Land He was taking them to would require a severing from the convenience of their past. It would require overcoming the ties to what they knew. He had to deliver them from yesterday in order to take them to a different tomorrow. And to do that, it required a bit of confusion in today.

As you meditate on the kingdom encounter made manifest at the Red Sea so many years ago, I want you to learn to look at your own dilemmas in a new way. Now, if you are in a dilemma and you are not in the will of God—that is a different lesson for a different day. But if you are in the will of God and you are facing a trickbag of sorts, then look to how God wants to use it get you to walk by faith. Let go of any complaining. I'm not saying to ignore the reality of what you face. If it's bad, it's bad. Don't call it good. But what I am encouraging you to do rather than complain, blame, or whine, is call out to God and ask Him to give you a bigger view of Him and His power than you have ever had before. Ask Him for your own kingdom encounter. Then watch Him roll back the waves and dry up the path so you can proceed to the next phase of your spiritual journey.

CHAPTER 3

Encountering God's Promises

There are times in our Christian experience when we don't always feel like God keeps His promises. That might not be something most of us are willing to admit publicly, but most of us have probably felt it nonetheless. There are times when it looks like God said one thing but the opposite is taking place. And it is during those times when most of us, to varying degrees, question how things really are.

When it comes to God's promises, we know the theological doctrine that God cannot lie. We understand that cognitively. God can't lie. But sometimes you may feel like He lied to you because what you felt and thought He said and what you are seeing simply do not match. They aren't coming together.

The story is told of a pilot who was flying a four-passenger plane when the engine began to have problems. Unfortunately, there was only one parachute on the plane. So the pilot took the parachute, went to the door, and turned to the four passengers. He said, "Don't panic. I'm just going to get some help."

Sometimes it may seem like the One who is in charge has bailed out on you. It may feel like His promises—designed to take you from point A to point B, or to right a wrong, or address a need—simply are not happening. They are not being fulfilled. A greater understanding of how God's promises work will help you as you go through these seasons of challenge and doubt. Encountering God's promises, like all other things, happens on God's terms—not ours.

As I've said before, God's ways are not our ways. His thoughts are higher than ours (Isa. 55:8–9). He is the great "unfiguroutable" God. But He has given us insight into how He works—especially with us as His creation—in His Word. By examining the principles and precepts laid out in His Word and applying them to our unique situations, we are able to navigate the unknowns of life in a spirit of peace, confidence, and clarity.

GOD TESTS

When you and I were in school, our teachers did not take our word for assessing what we learned. They didn't let us tell them whether we understood and remembered the lessons. They didn't just believe a student if he or she said, "I got it." Rather, they gave us tests.

The tests would usually come in two forms. One would be a quiz. This might even be a surprise "pop" quiz. The quizzes were small tests along the way. But then there were big ones, the mid-term and the final. Those tests typically carried the weight (or percentage) of your grade due to how large they were and how important they were in determining what was learned.

Scripture has tests in it as well. Yes, God tests His own. These tests are designed to reveal what has truly been learned, applicationally, versus what is just head knowledge. One of the biggest tests ever given in the Bible is recorded for us in Genesis 22. You are probably familiar with this story, so I want to caution you not to rush through it in your mind, assuming you have already grasped what there is to know. So much wisdom is found in this chapter that many people miss it simply because they feel they have already heard the story and choose to look no further.

When God wants to give you a kingdom encounter with Him, He will typically include a test. God may hear your "amens" you say in church or see you writing down your notes from your time in the Word, but none of that means anything until it is applied. Those who cook may know what I'm talking about when I say that the external appearance of something doesn't always reflect its true state internally. If you have a turkey in the oven, you don't take it out when it "looks" done. No, what you do is stick a thermometer into the center of it in order to determine if it really is done. A turkey may look good on the outside but still be raw and uncooked on the inside.

God knows His followers can easily look good on Sunday during church, but until He tests their heart by what they are willing to do, the truth of that person's transformation remains untold. Your kingdom encounter with God and His promises will always involve a test. But bear in mind, this is not just any kind of test because tests come in all shapes and sizes. No, this is a test related to a promise.

The tests we experience that are related to promises are unique. Typically, they are unique because they often involve a series of contradictions. A contradiction is when God says one thing but appears to be doing something else. It is when it looks as if God is doing the opposite of what He promised He would do. Which is why I say that these promise-based tests often involve contradictions.

FAITH DESPITE CONFUSION

The test we are about to explore, which took place in Genesis 22 concerning Abraham, didn't involve only one contradiction. This test was so big that it involved a number of contradictions—first of which was a theological contradiction. For starters, God had promised in Genesis 12 that He was going to make a great nation out of Abraham and that this nation would come through the son of Sarah. Fast-forward a bit to Genesis 22, and we read that God is asking Abraham to kill the promise:

> Now it came about after these things, that God tested Abraham, and said to him, "Abraham!" And he said, "Here I am." He said, "Take now your son, your only son, whom you love, Isaac, and go to the land of Moriah, and offer him there as a burnt offering on one of the mountains of which I will tell you." (vv. 1–2)

Did you catch the contradiction? Isaac was the one through

whom God said He would make a great nation. But Isaac was still a teenager. He is unmarried with no kids. How can he be used to make a great nation if he is dead? Abraham was faced with this question. He was faced with the theological conundrum of contradiction. How can he become a great nation if God is telling Abraham to kill the very promise God said the great nation would come through?

It seemed as if God was saying one thing all the while telling Abraham to do something else entirely. He was asked to kill what God had said should live.

But not only was this a theological contradiction for Abraham, it's also a biblical contradiction because God's command was not to commit murder. For Abraham to offer his son on the altar as a burnt offering could be done only if he killed him. Genesis 9:6 says, "Whoever sheds man's blood, by man his blood shall be shed, for in the image of God He made man." And later, God would reiterate this through Moses, "You shall not murder" (Ex. 20:13). Abraham knew those truths far better than most of us do today. This was central in his thinking. Yet God was asking him to contradict His own commands through sacrificing his son, no doubt casting thoughts of confusion in his mind.

This text included not only theological and biblical contradictions but also an emotional contradiction. As we read earlier in the passage, God told Abraham to sacrifice his "son, your only son, whom you love." Abraham loved Isaac. This was his only son through his wife, Sarah. He was the apple of his father's eye. And God was asking him to take the life of his only son, whom he loved. Abraham loved God. Abraham loved Isaac.

Obeying God meant betraying someone he loved. Preserving Isaac meant betraying Someone else he loved. There was no win in this contradiction, at least as far as the eye could see. Which is why it's always important that we never walk by sight but by faith. Because if what you see is all you see, then you will never see all there is to be seen.

The theological, biblical, and emotional contradictions plagued Abraham in this test. But there was one contradiction that remained—a spiritual contradiction. God had asked Abraham to offer up Isaac as a "burnt offering." A burnt offering, in Abraham's day, referred to an act of worship. God was asking Abraham not only to obey Him in the physical activity of a sacrifice, but also to worship Him through it. There's not a whole lot to say on that other than the obvious: that doesn't make sense!

But when God wants to give a person an encounter with Him at a kingdom level, the tests involved rarely make sense. The test will most often require the person to make the biggest decision of their lives in a situation where God looks like He doesn't know what He is doing. Perhaps this sounds familiar to you. Maybe you've been confused by God before. Maybe He's led you to do or say something that goes against the very things you thought about God. If you have, consider if that time or season in your life was God drawing you into an opportunity for obedience leading to a kingdom encounter.

These opportunities for obedience open doors for kingdom encounters to occur. In fact, a principle you'll want to remember is the greater the test, the more powerful the encounter (2 Cor. 1:8–10).

Abraham faced his own opportunity for obedience with this command to sacrifice his son. He faced a theological, biblical, emotional, and spiritual contradictory test. How Abraham responded in his test will give each of us insight in how we are to respond in our own. We read what he did in the face of this test in verse 3:

> So Abraham rose early in the morning and saddled his donkey and took two of his young men with him and Isaac his son; and he split wood for the burnt offering, and arose and went to the place of which God had told him.

Notice that Abraham rose "early." I believe Abraham got up early because he had to get out of there before Sarah woke up! He would have never been able to get out of that house to sacrifice her son if she was awake when he left. She would see that they did not have an animal sacrifice with them. She would inquire as to why. She would, most likely, put an end to the trip right then and there. Abraham knew better than let her see them, so he got up early enough to tiptoe out of the home and onto the path of their journey.

FAITH THAT REMEMBERS

Yet what I want us to know is what motivated Abraham to do this. What enabled him to find the courage to do something that made no sense at all? He wasn't a robot. He wasn't an unfeeling father out of touch with his emotions. The Scripture tells us that Isaac was the son whom Abraham loved. Abraham's obedience in this contradiction had to be rooted in something more than just a logical understanding of the request. Something had to be there to get him over the hump of fear, doubt, and trepidation. Thankfully, the writer of Hebrews answers this question for us. We read in Hebrews 11:17–19,

> By faith Abraham, when he was tested, offered up Isaac, and he who had received the promises was offering up his only begotten son; it was he to whom it was said, 'In Isaac your descendants shall be called.' He considered that God is able to raise people even from the dead, from which he also received him back as a type.

The reason Abraham was able to get up early, round up two of his servants, some animals, wood, and his son, and then head off to the place of the altar was because he had such confidence in God that faith triumphed over fear. Even if it didn't make sense to kill his son in light of all the obvious contradictions, Abraham knew that God would restore the situation some way. Even if it meant raising his son from the dead.

See, the bigger your view of God, especially in those times when He doesn't make sense, the better you are able to walk by faith. Abraham knew God could raise Isaac up. He was convinced of it. We hear his resolute faith in what he says to his servants as recorded in verse 5: "Abraham said to his young men, 'Stay here with the donkey, and I and the lad will go over there; and we will worship and return to you.'" Abraham told his servants that, following the sacrifice, they would return to them. You can return to someone only if you are alive enough to do so.

But where did Abraham get this great faith in God being able to raise the dead? Abraham learned firsthand of God's miraculous powers through the very conception and life of Isaac. After all, Sarah was ninety years old when she gave birth to Isaac. She had been barren all her life. Yet when Sarah had become advanced in years, God came to her and let her know that she would have a son. You might not be surprised to find out that Sarah laughed at the thought of it. Genesis 18:12 says, "Sarah laughed to herself, saying, 'After I have become old, shall I have pleasure, my lord being old also?'"

Not only did she doubt her own ability to conceive, but she doubted Abraham's physical ability in the process as well! She questioned both of them. Even so, at ninety years old, she conceived. A womb that had been dead for decades now held new life. Abraham experienced this miracle firsthand. If anyone should know that God can bring life out of death, it would be him. Abraham had learned from his history with God what God could do.

This is an important lesson for all of us. You have to remember what God did in your personal history with Him in order for it to help you with what you are dealing with at the moment.

Now, I understand, that's a problem if you've never had God do anything out of the norm for you—at least that you are aware of. If you read through the beginnings of the story of Abraham, you'll discover mistakes he made in failing to have faith in God. A huge one came when he doubted God's ability to produce life through the womb of Sarah, so he instead had a son through her maidservant Hagar. Thus, if you do not have your own past experiences with God, look to the experiences others have had whether in the Bible or in the body of Christ. Don't make the same mistakes Abraham made as he started his journey. But if you have experienced God's power in the past, you must rely on the recall of that power in order for it to produce even greater faith in you for future kingdom encounters as well.

That's what Abraham was able to do this time. Which is why he told his servants that he and Isaac would go and worship God and then return to them together. Isaac didn't have this history to rely on though so he questioned his father. It says in verses 7–8,

> Isaac spoke to Abraham his father and said, "My father!" And he said, "Here I am, my son." And he said, "Behold, the fire and the wood, but where is the lamb for the burnt offering?" Abraham said, "God will provide for Himself the lamb for the burnt offering, my son." So the two of them walked on together.

Abraham chose to answer Isaac in the only way he knew how. He pointed him to God. Then, as they arrived at the place of worship, Abraham proceeded to build the altar, arrange the wood, and then bind his son Isaac in order to lay him on top of the altar as a sacrifice. Can you imagine what he was thinking and feeling at that moment in time? None of this could have made sense. Abraham's hand is reaching for the knife all the while probably wondering what on earth is about to happen. His hand had to have been shaking while his stomach turned in knots.

Yet as Abraham lifted the knife to carry out the command God had given him, the "angel of the LORD" said, in my translation, "Enough!" Genesis 22:11–12 records it this way:

> "Abraham, Abraham!" And he said, "Here I am." He said, "Do not stretch out your hand against the lad, and do nothing to him; for now I know that you fear God, since you have not withheld your son, your only son, from Me."

You'll remember from our first chapter that the "angel of the LORD" is a type of Jesus Christ Himself. It is an appearance of our Lord and Savior. Just as Abraham is about to bring the knife down on his only son, the son he loves, God stops him. What's interesting, though, is what He says when He stops him. Did you catch it when you read the passage? He says, "now I know that you fear God."

The reason why this stands out as yet another contradiction in a test of contradictions is that God knows everything already. The doctrine of omniscience refers to God's all-knowingness. God knows all. There is nothing that sits outside of His knowledge. Anything that can be known is known by God. He knows all of the infinite details of any subject matter whether it was in the past, is in the present, or is to come. No one can throw God a surprise party! God never says, "Oops." He is fully aware of all things. In fact, not only does God know everything actual, He also knows everything potential. He knows what could have happened or could happen as well.

Yet even though God knows all things actual and potential, He does not know everything experiential. Let me put it another way: God has not experienced everything He knows. For example, if you were to ask God what it feels like to commit a sin, He couldn't tell you because He has never committed a sin. Although He knows all about sin and knows what it feels like to bear our sin, God has never sinned Himself. He doesn't know how it feels to sin because He has never sinned.

God has omniscience about the information regarding sin but not omniscience about the personal experience of that act. When God wanted to know what it feels like to be human, He became a man in the person of the Son. Hebrews 4:15 tells us that Christ did so in order to sympathize with our infirmities. He wanted to feel it. He wanted to feel loneliness, misuse, rejection, and the myriad of things we, as humans, experience on a regular basis but that God never did. Thus, He became one of us in order to experience much of what we experience ourselves.

So when the Angel of the Lord says, "Now I know that you fear God," it is not because He lacked any intellectual information but because He has now taken part in experiential participation. God enters into that moment in time when He experiences and feels the love we sing, speak, and think about.

"You say you'll give me your son?" God asks Abraham. "Now I know. Now I know that you fear Me. And I don't just know this as information, Abraham, because you could have stayed home for that. I know it experientially. You were willing to sacrifice what you loved more than anything else because of your love for and commitment to Me."

FAITH THAT ENCOUNTERS

One reason God puts you in a challenging situation such as a test is to give you the opportunity to enter into a relational encounter with Him. He does so by asking you to give up your own "Isaac." What is an "Isaac"? An "Isaac" is anything you love, treasure, or value most. God experiences your love for Him above the most valued thing in your life when your feet reveal your faith, especially when you obey without knowing in advance all the details.

Some promises God initiates and fulfills in His sovereignty simply because He has chosen to. But there are many promises—and I would dare to say the majority of them—that He does tied to what we do. God waits patiently on us to experience the level of our love and trust both for Him and in Him.

God wants to feel your love. He doesn't just want to hear it. He wants to feel it. Choosing Him over something you already love gives God the opportunity to feel it. When God wants to give you a kingdom encounter with Him, it will involve a contradiction that involves a choice. It may include having to choose to give up the thing you treasure most. But as bad as that seems, God is opening up the door for a kingdom encounter to take place.

What happened after the Angel of the Lord spoke to Abraham? We read on in verses 13–14,

> Then Abraham raised his eyes and looked, and behold, behind him a ram caught in the thicket by his horns; and Abraham went and took the ram and offered him up for a burnt offering in the place of his son. Abraham called the

name of that place The LORD Will Provide, as it is said to this day, "In the mount of the LORD it will be provided."

Little did Abraham know that all the while he was hiking up one side of the mountain, God was bringing his solution up the other side of the mountain. While Abraham climbed up the steep path, the ram climbed up the other side. Now, this had to have been the quietest ram in the history of all rams. If a ram is caught in a thicket, it has to be trying to wiggle to get out. But God kept the ram still. God kept the ram quiet. Abraham couldn't have seen or heard the ram ahead of time because God chose not to reveal what He was up to until obedience had been completed.

You see, a lot of us are looking for the ram when we haven't finished the obedience. As a result, God is keeping the ram quiet. The solution is already there. It just isn't revealed until after God experiences from us what He desires to experience. Far too often, we accuse God of not coming through for us when we are the ones who didn't do what He had said. Yet God didn't show Abraham anything until Abraham took the knife to slay his son. Abraham arising early in the morning wasn't enough. Abraham chopping the firewood wasn't enough. Abraham climbing the mountain wasn't enough.

God showed Abraham the ram when Abraham did what God had said. He will do the same thing for you when you completely do what He has asked you to do. You may be delaying the seeing of the ram because you are delaying the fulfilling of the obedience. Partial obedience is no obedience. God demands complete obedience. And until He sees that, the solution remains quiet.

But when He does see, He provides, just as the name Abraham ascribed to God boldly declares. When Abraham received the ram, he called the place "The Lord Will Provide." We know this today as the name "Jehovah Jireh." The Hebrew word for Jireh literally means to "to see beforehand." Thus, God provides when He sees. If you don't give Him something to see, you may not see what He can and will provide. His pre-vision leads to your provision.

After God provided Abraham with the ram, He called out to Abraham a second time in order to give him something more. We read about this in verses 16–18:

> "By Myself I have sworn, declares the LORD, because you have done this thing and have not withheld your son, your only son, indeed I will greatly bless you, and I will greatly multiply your seed as the stars of the heavens and as the sand which is on the seashore; and your seed shall possess the gate of their enemies. In your seed all the nations of the earth shall be blessed, because you have obeyed My voice."

In these three verses, we discover the distinction between God's promises and God's oaths. God had made a promise to Abraham decades before when He said He would make him a great nation (Gen. 12). But God doesn't swear by this promise until twenty-five years later as we see in Genesis 22. Decades had gone by without the fulfillment of the promise, but that is because God was waiting until Abraham was able to pass the test. See, between Genesis 12 and Genesis 22, Abraham made a bunch of mistakes. For one, he almost got his wife hooked up with another man (Gen. 20). He lied about her and said she was his sister. He also got another woman pregnant. Abe had a number of issues following God's promises to make a great nation out of him. Thus, God was not ready to give Abraham the fulfillment of His promise because Abraham was obviously not ready to handle it properly.

The principle is this: in the space between God's promise and God's oath—when He is prepared to fulfill His promise with nothing more required of you (Heb. 6:13–18)—is His preparation and development of you. Now, you have a part to play in how long that space lasts. Abraham chose to take roughly twenty-five years. Hopefully you won't take as long. God was not willing to swear by His oath regarding His promise until He saw Abraham obey Him out of a heart that trusted in Him when everything appeared to be a contradiction. Abraham no longer allowed his fears to rule his choices. Instead, he demonstrated great faith and in so doing, ushered in the oath to make a great nation through him.

James 2:22–23 takes it a step further than saying Abraham had great faith. James writes that Abraham perfected his faith. To perfect something is to make it complete or mature. We read,

> You see that faith was working with his works, and as a result of the works, faith was perfected; and the Scripture was fulfilled which says, "And Abraham believed God, and it was reckoned to him as righteousness," and he was called the friend of God.

Abraham's faith was made complete through this final act of total obedience and commitment to God. As a result, he transitioned from being just a child of God to a "friend of God." Now, that's a kingdom encounter we all want to have. It's easy to sing the popular Christian song, "Friend of God," but Scripture shows us it's not so easy to enter into that level of closeness and intimacy with the Most High God. If you want a similar level of closeness to God that ushers in the swearing of an oath to bring about the fulfillment of a divine promise, like Abraham had, then you also need to exhibit Abraham-level faith. This is a complete faith. A total faith. A faith that defies all logic. A faith that shuts down on all arguments. A faith that is countercultural. A faith that is willing to give up the very thing that means the most to you, what you love dearly, in order to demonstrate your love for the Lord.

One reason Abraham's story is such a well-known and retold story over and over again throughout history, and even today, is because within it lies the very principle to unlock what we all crave the most: closeness with our Creator. God felt Abraham's love through Abraham's actions. As a result, Abraham will forever be known as a friend of God (2 Chron. 20:7; Isa. 41:8). In addition, Abraham's obedience in this very difficult, challenging, and confusing test brought about the fulfillment of a several-decades-old promise through the sanction of an oath.

This physical illustration reveals to us a spiritual principle that ought to govern our choices and actions today. The author of Hebrews says that Abraham received Isaac back as a type (Heb. 11:19). This is when a physical reality becomes a personal, spiritual experience. It is the experience God wants to give to believers today. God still tests. He still desires to know how much you love and trust Him. He wants to see that you are developed to the point that you will act in faith and not just talk in faith. Jehovah Jireh is your provider. He's the great Provider. But He wants to see, first, your response to His leading and commands, especially in those times when you cannot figure out how in the world He is going to come through for you.

Trust Him. Obey Him. Honor Him. Encounter Him. The fulfillment of His promises are waiting for you.

Let me make one last vital observation. When Abraham was on his way to obey God, we are told that he "raised his eyes and saw the place from a distance" (22:4). When Jesus was defending His eternal deity to the Jewish leaders of His day, He stated that Abraham rejoiced to see His day and was glad (John 8:56). Mount Moriah, where Isaac was to be sacrificed, is a short distance from Calvary where Jesus was sacrificed. Abraham was able to obey a difficult command because he saw the preincarnate Christ. So when God calls you and me to trust and obey Him in a hard situation, keep your eyes on Jesus, the author and finisher of your faith (Heb. 12:1–3).

CHAPTER 4

Encountering God's Peace

One kingdom encounter sometimes comes on the heels of another kingdom encounter. The disciples discovered this just after they witnessed one of the greatest miracles in the Bible—the feeding of the multitude. Jesus had been teaching in a far-off location where the multitude had followed Him. Five thousand men were present, not counting women and children. The number must have been enormous. Jesus' compassion for the crowd moved Him to look for food for them. He first asked His disciples, but they said they didn't have enough food nor enough money to feed them. As far as they could see, they were right.

But Jesus wanted to teach them to see beyond what they could see. So He kept asking what they were going to feed them. That's when one disciple brought a small boy who had two fish and five barley loaves. After giving thanks for what seemingly looked to be not enough to feed a multitude, Jesus gave the disciples the instruction to pass out the food to everyone. And they did just that. In fact, not only did the food remain plentiful in feeding the entire multitude, but there also remained twelve baskets of food when they were done—what I like to think of as a bag for each disciple, a momento of this miraculous event displaying God's ability to provide.

The people were so excited about what they had witnessed that they rushed to make Jesus king. Yet the Scripture tells us that Jesus left. He left because He knew they didn't really want to make Him king, but what they wanted was more like a burger king. They had seen His physical provision and wanted to tap into that. They wanted Him for what He would give them. They wanted a "Bless Me" club, a social program without a spiritual Savior.

But even so, the miracle had served its purposes. First, to feed the people. Secondly, to teach the disciples.

God had wanted the disciples to see His power over the material world and to recognize His compassion for those in need. But based on the next kingdom encounter the disciples were about to head into, it's doubtful they learned that lesson.

Shortly after the massive feeding, Jesus told the disciples to get into a boat and head to the other side of the Sea. Jesus chose to remain on the land. Picture it: Jesus sends His disciples away at night. But He stays behind. He goes to pray. Then a storm pops up out of nowhere and the wind becomes fierce. It battered the sides of the boat. It tossed the disciples like toys played with by a child. There was nothing they could do to get out of the storm. Every inch of headway they thought they made, the storm twisted and thwarted their progress. They were stuck. In a storm.

I like how the Scripture explains the wind to us. It says the wind was contrary (Matt. 14:24). The NIV words it this way: "the boat was already a considerable distance from land, buffeted by the waves because the wind was against it." The wind worked against the disciples' attempts at extracting themselves from the storm. It's as if the wind had a mind of its own. The disciples wanted to go one way, and the wind sought to take them the other way. They would try to go east, and the wind would drive them west. Then they would try to go north, and the wind would push them south. They were stuck in the middle of the storm with no way out while trying to obey their Master.

I imagine the disciples must have been confused. After all, Jesus, who had just demonstrated miraculous power over the material world through feeding the multitude, had told them to get into the boat. He had told them to go over to the other side. They were obeying Him. Yet He sent them straight into a storm. If they had a moment to think while they were battling the waves, I wouldn't be surprised if their thoughts were wrapped in confusion.

Maybe this sounds familiar to you. Maybe you've tried to follow what God led you to do. Or maybe you heard His words to you and sought to obey Him only to find yourself worse off than when you weren't following Him at all. Everything you seek to do is faced with opposition. It's as if the world itself is conspiring against you all the while you are seeking to obey God. That can lead to high levels of confusion for anyone. Which is why it's always important to return to the Scriptures when doubt raises its head in our hearts.

FINDING THE PURPOSE OF THE STORM

When God allows a storm in your life, He does it for a purpose. Now, the purpose may not be the same for all of us at the same time. For example, the purpose of this storm in the disciples' lives wasn't the same purpose as the storm God sent to track down Jonah when he sought to run away from His presence. But whatever the purpose may be, look for it. Because when God sends a storm, He is attempting to work in you, through you, or around you—either to correct or perfect something. God wants to fix something that may be broken or develop something that may need to grow.

Jesus deliberately placed His disciples in the storm. Even though it may not have felt like it to the disciples, they were smack dab in the middle of where God wanted them to be. And what's more, they were alone. At least they felt alone. Last time they were in a storm, Jesus had been with them, sleeping on a pillow. But this time, Jesus had chosen to go off by Himself and pray. He was doing what we read about in Hebrews 7:25, "Therefore he [Jesus] is able to save completely those who come to God through him, because he always lives to intercede for them" (NIV). He was praying for His disciples.

If we look elsewhere in Scripture, we can gain insight into what Jesus is praying. In Luke 22, we come across another situation where Jesus is praying for one of His disciples. Peter has just told Jesus that no matter who betrays Him, he never would. But Jesus knows better. And Jesus knows what was more important in the long run, and that is the retaining of Peter's faith in the midst of Peter's failure. Because personal failure can often lead to a landslide of lost esteem, which then produces a lack of faith and confidence. Jesus told Peter what was the most important thing when He said,

> "Simon, Simon, Satan has asked to sift all of you as wheat. But I have prayed for you, Simon, that your faith may not fail. And when you have turned back, strengthen your brothers." (Luke 22:31–32 NIV)

Jesus prayed that Peter's faith would not fail. Likewise, when Jesus prays for you as you go through a storm, He is praying that your faith might remain strong in spite of the circumstances that He Himself has allowed you to be placed in. He is praying for the strengthening and development of your faith. Trials are designed to cause you to trust Him more. Thus, when storms are splashing all around you—whether they be financial, relational, professional, or any other type of storm, especially one that involves a contradiction—it is God attempting to develop greater faith in you. He wants you to have a kingdom encounter that will expand your knowledge of Him, belief in Him, and compassion for others who also need to grow in faith.

SEEING JESUS IN THE STORM

Jesus didn't just sit on the mountain praying generally while the disciples struggled in the storm. He prayed specifically. Then around the fourth watch of the night—somewhere between three and six in the morning—He had finished praying and decided to come to the disciples in the storm. He came to them walking on the water.

Now, keep in mind that during a storm, the moon is blacked out. There is no light anywhere. Pitch blackness swarms around the disciples like the waves slamming the sides of the boat. When Jesus walked toward them, they couldn't see Him at first. But in the darkness, distance, and disruption around them, He chose to enter into their trial from a most unusual place. The waters are contrary. The sea is storming. The sea itself is the problem. But Jesus didn't first appear to them in a way that fixed their problem. Rather, He chose to appear to them while walking on their problem. Jesus came to them on top of their problem. Nothing had changed. He just chose to walk on top of the circumstances seeking to bring them down. As Isaiah 43:2 says, "When you pass through the waters, I will be with you; and when you pass through the rivers, they will not sweep over you" (NIV).

The gospel of Mark gives us more insight into the situation on the sea. In Mark's writings, it tells us that the disciples were straining at the oars. The disciples were putting forth enormous human effort in an attempt to save themselves. No doubt they were grunting and groaning in this desperate situation. But every move forward resulted in two moves backward because the wind was against them. The wind was their enemy, and the wind had more strength than they did.

Mark also tells us something about Jesus' intentions that the other accounts do not. It says that when Jesus was walking on the water, He intended to pass them by. We read, "He saw the disciples straining at the oars, because the wind was against them.

Shortly before dawn he went out to them, walking on the lake. He was about to pass by them" (6:48 NIV). Jesus had gotten close enough to them for them to react to Him, but He wasn't going to force Himself into their situation. He intended to pass them by.

But returning to Matthew's account, we can see the disciple's reaction when he writes, "When the disciples saw him walking on the lake, they were terrified. 'It's a ghost,' they said, and cried out in fear" (Matt. 14:26 NIV). Now, these disciples were already afraid of the storm. But to see something that appears to be a ghost walking on the water in the midst of the storm took it all to the next level. They were a scared group of men. They were straining and screaming and, because of all the focus on their own effort and fears, they didn't even recognize it was Jesus walking on the water toward them. It didn't even dawn on them to look for Jesus in the middle of the mess they found themselves in. He could have walked back and forth in front of them a dozen times, and they may have never recognized Him.

I'm curious how many times Jesus has been near to you when you were in the middle of a personal storm, and you didn't recognize Him. Could it be that your focus was too closely tied to the circumstances that you failed to recognize His face? Unfortunately, far too many of us miss our kingdom encounters because we are fixated on what we are worried about rather than on the solution for our problem, which is always Jesus. If you are not looking for Jesus, you will not see Him. Even if He comes walking on the waves. He could be right by your boat, and you'd miss Him entirely.

The disciples almost did. They were full of fear. They yelled.

They screamed. They cried out that it was a ghost. But when Jesus saw their fear, He brought them calm. Before He could even address the waves, He had to still the storm within them first. We read in verse 27, "'But Jesus immediately said to them: "Take courage! It is I. Don't be afraid"'" (NIV).

Jesus knew He had to address their fears before anything else could happen. They needed to hear His voice above the roar of the waves and the crashing against the sides of the boat. The reason is because He needed them to have faith. But fear negates faith. Fear cancels out faith, causing you to be blind to Jesus. Now, I understand that fear is a normal emotion that comes whenever something concerning happens in your life. But fear will not accomplish anything for you. Fear simply turns into worry. And worry is a lot like a rocking chair. It keeps you moving but gets you nowhere.

Thus, whenever you feel fear, that is a signal. It is your clue to look to God and listen to Him. He is calling you to an act of faith. When you do, you will hear His voice—like the disciples did—telling you to take courage. We can never guess what God is going to do to reverse negative circumstances in our lives, but what we can predict is what He is going to say. He will always tell us to fear not, take courage, and focus on Him. The disciples were not alone in the darkness of that storm. Neither are you alone in whatever you are going through right now. Jesus is there. Walking on the circumstances that are scaring you. He is telling you to take courage, trust Him, and turn your fear into faith.

EXERCISING FAITH IN THE STORM

Peter was the first to allow his fears to be overcome by faith. He called back to Jesus and asked Him to tell him to come to Him on the water. He wanted to know it was Him. He wanted to experience his kingdom encounter right then and there. Peter is a type A personality. He will try anything. He is also no dummy. He knew that boat was going nowhere. He knew the boat was taking on water. It was dark. He was soaked. But Jesus stood on top of the water that threatened to consume him. Not only that, Jesus is walking on the water with intention of passing them by, meaning the boat had made no progress. The boat was still in one location because the winds kept beating it back into submission. But Jesus was making progress. He could walk to the other shore if He wanted to do so.

The disciples had been straining and huffing and puffing as they tried to make progress toward the shore. But Jesus was walking, casually, as if it were easy. Peter wanted a piece of that. Peter wanted to experience that. Peter wanted out of the boat. So Jesus told him to get out and come. Now, I don't know about you, but my heart would have been racing when Jesus told me to get out of the boat. My thoughts would have been questioning my sanity. I may have asked Jesus to repeat Himself, just to be sure. But not Peter. The Bible tells us that Peter got right out of the boat and started to head toward Jesus. We read, "Then Peter got down out of the boat, walked on the water and came toward Jesus" (v. 29 NIV).

The actual occurrence of Peter walking on water was probably a lot different from what has been portrayed in picture books and movies. Typically, we see Peter striding along on a few waves here or there. But this storm was bad. These waves were furious. It was probably difficult to even spot Peter in the water. And as far as what he could see, where should he step? It might look like a part of a wave was good for stepping on in one moment, but bad the next. It was a constant-changing situation, and the water was anything but smooth.

Yet he took the step of faith. The problem was he still had his fear. Peter hadn't left his fear in the boat. Fear and faith don't mix well, as Peter found out. Seeing the wind and the waves splashing all around him, he took his eyes off Jesus and began to sink. The moment he shifted his focus from Christ to his circumstances, he started to go under. One moment he was walking with Jesus on top of his problem. The next moment, Jesus was still walking there, but he was sinking.

Sound familiar? If you are sinking in your circumstances, you've lost your focus. If you are feeling overwhelmed by all that rages on around you, you are paying the wind and the waves too much attention. I'm not saying you should ignore the circumstances. I'm not recommending that you act like there is no storm. The issue at hand doesn't involve the presence of the problem. The issue is what authority does that problem have over your life? Are you spending your time looking at the problem, trying to solve the problem, analyzing the problem, and worrying about the problem? Or are you resting in the calm and confidence Christ has given you to enable you to walk on top of your problem rather than be swallowed up by it?

Most of us spend our time running from our circumstances

only to discover that the wind remains with us. The wind continues to torment us. And it does so because God has allowed the difficulties for a reason. That reason is that you will learn to depend on Him while giving up your self-sufficiency. He wants you to stop straining at the oars. He wants you to breathe freely. He wants you to focus your attention on His authority rather than all the other things that seek to sink you down.

After Peter started sinking, he called out to Jesus to save him. That had to be the shortest prayer in the history of prayers. But the length of our prayers do not matter as much as the heart behind them. Because as soon as he prayed it, Jesus reached out to save him. The passage tells us it was immediate. We read, "Immediately Jesus reached out his hand and caught him. 'You of little faith,' he said, 'why did you doubt?'" (v. 32 NIV).

As Jesus rescued Peter from drowning, He reminded him what had caused him to sink. It was his little faith. Peter had just come from the miracle where Jesus demonstrated His power over the material world by feeding the multitude. But even with that history, Peter doubted. Even with seeing the authority of God up close and personal, Peter wavered. Jesus knew his faith was enough to keep him from going under. But Peter decided to focus more on the problem than on the face of Jesus. Yes, he had great faith when he had stepped out of the boat. But he went from great faith to little faith in a matter of seconds.

The difference between great faith and little faith is the object of focus. If you look at Jesus, and Him alone, your faith will be great. If you look at your circumstances, it will be small. Where you choose to focus will determine your faith. Never focus on the storm. The storm cannot save you. Always look at the One who holds the power over the storm. Stop giving your circumstances that much attention. If Jesus tells you to "come," then trust He will give you all you need to get there. If Jesus tells you to get in the boat and cross over to the other side, then He will give you all you need to cross over. Whatever God calls you to do, He will do. Trust Him. He is not going to ask you to step out in faith only to leave you hanging.

Peter learned this through the lessons of his trials. That's why he wrote about faith in his epistle. In 1 Peter 1:6–7, he gives us the wisdom he learned:

> In all this you greatly rejoice, though now for a little while you may have had to suffer grief in all kinds of trials. These have come so that the proven genuineness of your faith—of greater worth than gold, which perishes even though refined by fire—may result in praise, glory and honor when Jesus Christ is revealed. (NIV)

Trials prove the genuineness, or lack, of your faith. Peter reminds us in this passage that faith is greater than gold because faith results in praise, glory, and honor when Jesus Christ is revealed. Jesus gave Peter a kingdom encounter of such magnitude because Jesus wanted Peter to see that he still had room to grow. Peter would later be used as a great instrument in the growth of the church, but he would need stronger faith before he could reach that point. This kingdom encounter showed him how much further he still needed to go.

One good thing to note is that even though this kingdom

encounter included much fear, straining, and difficulties for not only Peter, but also all the disciples, it concluded with calm. We read, "And when they climbed into the boat, the wind died down. Then those who were in the boat worshiped him, saying, 'Truly you are the Son of God'" (vv. 32–33 NIV). The wind stopped. The calm resumed. Jesus' presence in the boat turned reckless waters into a restful sea. What's more, John's writing about this miracle tells us that once the disciples received Jesus into the boat, "immediately the boat reached the shore where they were heading" (John 6:21 NIV). Immediately they reached their destination. They were suddenly at the place they were supposed to be.

God's authority can not only calm the chaos in your heart and life but also usher you directly into the place you were meant to be all along. But in order for Him to do that, you need to live by faith. You need to focus on Jesus. You need to receive Jesus into whatever situation you are in. Once you do, His power will produce peace both in and for you.

Let Jesus walk with you in the storms life brings your way. When you do, you will experience a kingdom encounter designed to take your faith to an all-new level. You will discover the perfection of His peace.

CHAPTER 5

Encountering God's Provision

A building had caught fire in a large city. A man clung for dear life as he struggled to breathe while trapped inside. Yet another man—some people know him as the Man of Steel—whisked in, grabbed this trapped man who was in danger of being consumed by the fire, and lifted him out of there. As the Man of Steel began to fly and lift the man from the fire high up into the safety of the sky, the man who had been delivered became very afraid. This was higher than he had ever been, outside of the protection of an airplane, of course.

Superman sensed the man's fear. After all, the man was shaking. So that's when he questioned him, "What makes you think I could deliver you from the fire but cannot hold onto you after I've set you free?"

That's a good question—not only for that man, but for all of us. Because if you are a believer in Jesus Christ by placing your faith alone in Christ alone for the forgiveness of your sins and the free gift of eternal life, He has delivered you from the eternal fire. You have been set free from the flames. But what makes you think that the God who delivered you from the fire can't take care of you now that He has set you free? What makes you doubt that the God who rescued you for eternity cannot hold onto you in time?

We serve a powerful God. Let's stop insulting His power with our doubt and fear.

As you experience more kingdom encounters with God over the course of your life, you will come to know His power both for eternity and the present time. This intimate awareness of God Himself will enable you to live with the courage necessary to obey Him even when fear pervades your soul. In our next scriptural example of a divine kingdom encounter, we are going to look at one woman who did just that. Her story piggybacks off our last story involving Abraham because this is a story of provision. And as we saw with the name Jehovah Jireh, meaning "God Sees Beforehand," God will often wait to see our obedience before He provides.

REASONS FOR NO PROVISION

Have you ever asked the question: Why does God allow us to be in circumstances where it looks like He is not providing? I am certain there are many people reading this book who have asked that at one time or another. It's a human question. We are shaped by what we experience and see, far too often limiting our understanding to our five senses. It's okay to admit that you've asked that question before, or even if you are still asking it now. Maybe you feel like God has let you down. Or maybe you feel that God has left you out. Maybe you feel that He didn't come through for you when you needed Him to. Instead of providing for you, He seemed to be taking His time and ignoring the reality you were facing.

There are a number of reasons why God allows His people to enter circumstances where provision is lacking. One reason involves our own fault. Deuteronomy 11:16–17 tells us that when we make something or someone else into an idol, God will hold back His provision. It says,

> "Beware that your hearts are not deceived, and that you do not turn away and serve other gods and worship them. Or the anger of the LORD will be kindled against you, and He will shut up the heavens so that there will be no rain and the ground will not yield its fruit; and you will perish quickly from the good land which the LORD is giving you."

God spoke these words to the Israelites at a time when they were entirely an agricultural nation. In any agricultural nation, rain is critical. Were God to "shut up the heavens so that there will be no rain," He would be allowing them to experience lack. But this particular lack was tied to a particular sin: idolatry.

Now, an *idol* isn't always a wood carving hung on string or a statue in a temple. No, an idol can be many things. An idol is any noun—person, place, thing, or thought—that you set up in your heart as having more authority and value than God. It is any noun that you appeal to as your source of meaning, pleasure, security, finances, and more. It could be as seemingly innocent as a television show or social media to something more harmful as a toxic relationship or the love of money. God told Israel plainly that if they were to set up any competing entities with Him, then He would let them rely on that competition for their provision.

When we abandon God through our own sinful marginalization of His rightful place in our hearts, minds, and souls, we are walking away from the Provider. Through our own sin, we are stopping our own provision. Thus, one reason provision may be lacking is because God has been abandoned. When the Israelites turned from God and toward idols, such as Ba'al, He left them to provide their own resources for themselves. If and when God is no longer appealed to, respected, and followed as Jehovah Jireh, He often no longer manifests this attribute in a person's or nation's experience.

Another reason why God allows for a lack of provision in our lives is because He is testing us. Deuteronomy 8:1–3 explains it this way:

> "All the commandments that I am commanding you today you shall be careful to do, that you may live and multiply, and go in and possess the land which the LORD swore to give to your forefathers. You shall remember all the way which the LORD your God has led you in the wilderness these forty years, that He might humble you, testing you, to know what was in your heart, whether you would keep His commandments or not. He humbled you and let you

be hungry, and fed you with manna which you did not know, nor did your fathers know, that He might make you understand that man does not live by bread alone, but man lives by everything that proceeds out of the mouth of the LORD."

An easy way to understand this concept in our contemporary culture is through what is known as a stress test. When a person goes to the doctor for a stress test, the doctor or nurses intentionally put the patient's body under stress so they can see the true state of the patient's health. One of the ways God lets you know the true state of your spiritual growth and development is through trials and stress. You may talk a great Christian game, but the truth comes out when you are experiencing lack or challenging situations.

In the above passage, God let the Israelites go hungry so their hearts could be tested and they would be humbled. He did it to help them get rid of their perceived self-sufficiencies. One reason God will allow lack—whether emotional, physical, financial, professional, or even spiritual—is to strike a deathblow to our independence. God hates pride. He hates it when you feel like you can make it without Him. Why? Because the truth is you can't. I can't. None of us can. But we grow comfortable and proud in His provision, confusing it for our own, and that's when He needs to teach us a lesson. He does this by not allowing your contacts to come through, or the promotion to come through, or your savings to get depleted over one thing breaking after another. He will allow lack in order to grow you to the point where you realize your one—and only—Source is Him.

On your best day, and on my best day, you and I are dependent on God—for everything.

The great apostle Paul had to be reminded of this as well. In 2 Corinthians 1:8–10, he explains what God was teaching him through hardship and lack:

> For we do not want you to be unaware, brethren, of our affliction which came to us in Asia, that we were burdened excessively, beyond our strength, so that we despaired even of life; indeed, we had the sentence of death within ourselves so that we would not trust in ourselves, but in God who raises the dead; who delivered us from so great a peril of death, and will deliver us, He on whom we have set our hope. And He will yet deliver us.

Paul said God allowed him and his fellow gospel workers to get so low in order to deepen their faith and fully learn what it means to trust God. God will allow us to get into circumstances we cannot fix, even when we are in His will, in order to take us to a deeper level of experience with and trust in Him. But if you don't know that truth, then you will just get mad at God when things go wrong. You will question God when things don't add up. You will also get frustrated at life and those around you, rather than mine the spiritual strength and dependency God has planned for you to access through the absence of provision.

GOD ALONE IS YOUR SOURCE

This one principle that I'm going to share with you in this chapter has been the most revolutionary principle I've ever learned. I learned it years ago through life experiences that God allowed me to face, and also through the wise teaching of a spiritual friend. The principle is this: God (alone) is your Source. You only have one Source. As simple as that sounds, it is life transforming when you truly understand it. You cannot have multiple sources. Anything outside God is a resource. It is not a source. It's merely a vehicle of provision. The grocery store is not your source. It's merely a resource you go to. They don't make the food. They sell the food. It's not your source. It's a channel through which you get something rather than the origination of the something you get.

Your job is not your source. It is a resource through which God Himself provides. Over and over again in Scripture, the Bible declares that God is our only Source. In Psalm 104:1–17, God tells us that the animals eat only because He feeds them, the birds eat only because He feeds them, and people eat only because He feeds us. God boldly declares in this passage, and others, that He is our Source. He is our starting point. There is no other.

Whenever you treat a resource as though it were the source, you have made it an idol. For some people, their job is an idol. Or their bank account is an idol. Even their contacts can be an idol. Or their education. Whatever is viewed or relied on as a source other than God instantly becomes an idol.

God is your Source. And until you establish that principle

in your heart and mind as truth, you will always be controlled by either the presence or absence of a resource. Because when your resources go left on you, or your friends go left on you, or your health goes left on you, you will succumb to worry, doubt, dread, and despair. But when you recognize God as your one and only Source, circumstances do not have to ultimately dictate your emotions or actions.

One reason this truth is so important, and why it's so freeing for me personally, is that when you come to understand and believe it, you will no longer be controlled by anyone or anything. No one can own you. If God is your Source and your resources turn sour, you are still not controlled because you were never depending on your resources to begin with. They were merely a mechanism through which God was choosing to provide. But God has a million mechanisms, and then some, through which He can provide. He used a raven to feed His prophet Elijah, after all, and ravens were even classified as "unclean" birds in Israelite culture (1 Kings 17:2–16). God doesn't need our permission to use whatever resource He chooses to. Which is also why it's never wise to box God into our own understanding. He can hit a bull's-eye with a crooked stick. His ways are higher than ours. His provision can often come through unexpected and unknown channels. Just like it did for a widow in a town named Zarephath, in the region of Sidon.

Now, I'm from Dallas, where a church exists on every street corner—and then some. Texas is in the Bible Belt of America. But Zaraphath was in what could be called the Ba'al Belt. It was in the center of Ba'al worship. Idolatry, in its most grotesque forms, was rampant everywhere. But in the midst of this do-main of debauchery, God sent His prophet Elijah to get a meal. God was sending Elijah not only into the heart and veins of Ba'al worshipers but also to a widow who was running out of food. If that didn't get a prophet to scratch his head, I don't know what would. That seems like an unusual request. Elijah may have wondered whether he had heard God right.

But God always prepares us for His prompts. Consider the ravens I mentioned just a couple paragraphs ago. In that passage, God had sent ravens to take food to Elijah when he was on the run from his enemies. We read in 1 Kings 17:4, "It shall be that you will drink of the brook, and I have commanded the ravens to provide for you there." Here we have a seemingly enormous spiritual contradiction.

In Deuteronomy 14:11–14 it says, "You may eat any clean bird. But these are the ones which you shall not eat: the eagle and the vulture and the buzzard, and the red kite, the falcon, and the kite in their kinds, and every raven in its kind." Elijah knew this list. He knew the ravens were considered unclean. Yet God spe-cifically sent ravens to bring him bread and meat. And while Eli-jah didn't violate God's command against eating ravens because the ravens brought him food to eat, he did experience a greater glimpse into God's ability to use whatever means or methods He chooses to provide. God can use the evil to make provisions for His people. He can use the unclean to answer a prayer. God had said not to eat the ravens in His Word. He never said that they couldn't be used.

One of the key kingdom principles for spiritual growth is

knowing that God has the right to do as He pleases. While He is never inconsistent with Himself, He can go beyond our finite understanding to accomplish His purposes, even if it involves using the evil that exists in order to do so. God can use the devil to answer your prayers. That's how big of a God He is. Now, before you close this book too quickly, let me give you a biblical example. Do you know how the Israelites got all of the money they had when they left Egypt? They had no money. They were slaves. But God used the Egyptians to give them the money they needed to flee from slavery and pursue national freedom. We read about this in Exodus 12:35–36:

> Now the sons of Israel had done according to the word of Moses, for they had requested from the Egyptians articles of silver and articles of gold, and clothing; and the Lord had given the people favor in the sight of the Egyptians, so that they let them have their request. Thus, they plundered the Egyptians.

The Israelites plundered the Egyptians in the most unusual manner. They asked for it. Thus, God used Egypt to finance Israel's escape from Egypt in order to fulfill His command of letting them go. Similarly, do you know how Jerusalem got rebuilt and paid for after it had been demolished during Old Testament times? In the book of Nehemiah, we read that the King of Persia provided Nehemiah safe passage and funding to rebuild his land (Neh. 1–3). God is so good at providing that even the devil has to hand over money when God calls for it. And Proverbs 13:22 says, "the wealth of the sinner is stored up for the righteous."

Your view of your boss or the people in your vicinity who seem to oppose you has to take into perspective the truth that God alone sits as King, Judge, and Jury. We see this time and again in Scripture:

"I am the Lord, and there is no other; besides Me there is no God." (Isa. 45:5)

There is only one Lawgiver and Judge, the One who is able to save and to destroy. (James 4:12)

But God is the Judge; He puts down one and exalts another. (Ps. 75:7)

The king's heart is like channels of water in the hand of the Lord; He turns it wherever He wishes. (Prov. 21:1)

"See now that I, I am He, and there is no god besides Me; It is I who put to death and give life. I have wounded and it is I who heal, and there is no one who can deliver from My hand." (Deut. 32:39)

"Yet I have been the Lord your God since the land of Egypt; and you were not to know any god except Me, for there is no savior besides Me." (Hos. 13:4)

God alone is God. Which is exactly why we are to look to Him, and Him alone, as our Source—even if what He is asking us to do doesn't make sense. I'm sure the thought of going into the heart of hedonism and Ba'al worship to ask a starving widow for some food caused Elijah to pause and wonder whether he had misheard God. But since Elijah had a history with God like he did, he didn't pause long. He knew that God functioned outside of our expectations. God is not limited to our limiting logic. It is interesting to note that God did not give Elijah direction on His next method of provision until the previous one dried up (1 Kings 17:7–9). God knows the right time to lead us to what is next. So, Elijah went. He obeyed God and went searching for a meal from a most unusual person in a most uncomfortable location. When he got there, he found the widow and asked her for some bread.

The widow's initial response shouldn't surprise us. She said,

> "As the LORD your God lives, I have no bread, only a handful of flour in the bowl and a little oil in the jar; and behold, I am gathering a few sticks that I may go in and prepare for me and my son, that we may eat it and die." (1 Kings 17:12)

She hesitated, pretty strongly. Letting Elijah know that she was down to her very last meal, and the very last meal for her son, she pushed back. This came even though God had commanded her to feed the prophet (1 Kings 17:9). Not only was Elijah's faith tested in having to go where he went and ask for food from the least suspecting person, but the widow's faith was also tested. How could she feed the prophet if she couldn't even feed herself?

But her story reflects many of our own. It may not be that we are down to our last meal, but when difficulties and trials come, we can certainly feel like we are down to our last option.

But those are the times we need to open our eyes in search of a kingdom encounter. Because often when God wants to reveal Himself through His provision, it will be at a point of your deepest inconvenience. It will frequently be at a point where you don't even know how you are going to take care of anything at all. You will have hit rock bottom.

But God does some of His best work in those times when we don't feel like He is doing anything at all. When you feel trapped, hopeless, worn out, and lost, look to God. In those times, He's asking you to focus your attention on Him. Obey Him. Trust Him. Do the very thing you need the most. God will often look to see whether you are willing to obey Him out of your lack because that demonstrates a kingdom heart.

Scripture tells us about this cause and effect occurrence many times:

> "Give, and it will be given to you." (Luke 6:38)

> The generous man will be prosperous, and he who waters will himself be watered. (Prov. 11:25)

> "When you reap your harvest in your field and have forgotten a sheaf in the field, you shall not go back to get it; it shall be for the alien, for the orphan, and for the widow, in order that the LORD your God may bless you in all the work of your hands." (Deut. 24:19)

> For the one who sows to his own flesh will from the flesh reap corruption, but the one who sows to the Spirit will from the Spirit reap eternal life. (Gal. 6:8)

You don't plant corn to get potatoes. You plant corn to get corn. Similarly, the very thing you need—or the very place you are experiencing the greatest lack—is often the very thing God is going to ask you to step toward with faith. People who need a relationship ought to be willing to give a relationship—whether that's visiting the shut-in or elderly, or reaching out to their own family more than they do. People who lack provision need to be willing to give provision to others who need it too. God wants faith demonstrated, not just discussed. The widow was down to her last meal. She had one day left to live. So God asked her to give away her last meal. Which, after putting up a bit of a fuss, she chose to do—after Elijah sought to reassure her that she would not run out. We read about this in 1 Kings 17:13–14:

> Then Elijah said to her, "Do not fear; go, do as you have said, but make me a little bread cake from it first and bring it out to me, and afterward you may make one for yourself and for your son. For thus says the LORD God of Israel, 'The bowl of flour shall not be exhausted, nor shall the jar of oil be empty, until the day that the LORD sends rain on the face of the earth.'"

Elijah knew the widow was afraid. He also knew she had every right to be afraid. That's why he sought to calm her fears. Elijah didn't scold her for her fear. He honored the reality of the emotion while simultaneously encouraging the courage to overcome it.

Unfortunately, too many Christians today limit themselves to their five senses. They don't live in the spiritual. They live only in the five senses of the visible, material world. So they never get to see what an encounter with God feels like. But when the widow allowed her faith to overcome her feelings, as demonstrated by the fact that she did as the prophet and God asked her to do, it says that she got her provision. We read,

> So she went and did according to the word of Elijah, and she and he and her household ate for many days. The bowl of flour was not exhausted nor did the jar of oil become empty, according to the word of the LORD which He spoke through Elijah. (vv. 15–16)

In other words, God stretched it. He took the little that was there and made it last. Until the rain could fall again in order to provide sufficient food, God provided supernaturally for her, her son, and Elijah. Jesus even used her as an object lesson of faith to the Jewish leaders of His day who heard Him teach when He announced the inauguration of His public ministry (Luke 4:24–27).

All throughout Scripture, there are stories of God stretching the supernatural provision to meet people's needs. Whether it was through water from a rock or a feast from some sardines, God knows how to stretch humanity's resources in such a way to make them sufficient for what we need. For you to truly experience a kingdom encounter with God as your provider, you must look beyond the physical to the spiritual. You must be willing to give out of your lack, if He asks you to do so. And you must always remember, and respect, that God alone is your Source. He is the One providing for you. He's the One taking care of you.

Keep your eyes on the living God, especially when you are the most tempted to remove them. He is there. He does care. He heals. Gives. Restores. Stretches. Provides. Redeems. And more. He knows just what you need and when you need it most. Trust Him. Trust the process. If you do, you will be able to say like David, "The LORD is my shepherd, I shall not want" (Ps. 23:1).

CHAPTER 6

Encountering God's Promotion

The story is told of a bird who flew south for the winter to get away from the harsh cold. The bird had started too late and found itself caught in a tremendous blizzard. Its wings began to freeze and weigh it down. Finally, the bird could fly no more and came crashing to the ground.

As the bird lay there frozen and unable to move, along came a cow. The cow just so happened to relieve itself on top of the bird. Now the bird was not only frozen but also stinky. The situation appeared to have gone from bad to worse. Yet in the midst of that, something good began to happen. The warmth of the manure began to melt the ice on the bird. Thus, a stinky situation reversed a frozen situation. The bird got so excited about the ice melting that it began to sing for joy. Yet the singing drew attention to him, and along came a cat who ate the bird.

There are a couple of lessons in this story. The first is obvious. Everything that puts manure on your life may not be your enemy. But another lesson is when you find yourself delivered because of a manure pile, keep your mouth shut!

There are some people reading this book who feel like their life has been covered in manure. They feel like they are not only in a dirty situation, but also frozen stuck. It seems that no matter what they try to get ahead, things just keep getting worse. Perhaps you feel that way. As we continue to look at kingdom encounters in Scripture, I want you to see that oftentimes your greatest encounter with God will be when things are not right.

Your kingdom encounter will often come when it appears that God is nowhere to be found. It has been said that Christians are like tea bags. You know how strong they are only when they are put in hot water. But I'd like to change the wording on that so it's more accurate. Many Christians do not know how strong God is until they are in hot water. Or, even more so, hot flames.

Such was the case of Shadrach, Meshach, and Abed-nego, as we read in Daniel 3. On their way to experiencing a kingdom promotion, they first must past through the fire.

Let's start with the backdrop of their story.

WHOM WE SERVE

The three young men have found themselves working in a pagan society. They are in Babylon. Babylon is an evil, idolatrous country. Because of Israel's sin, God told Babylon to invade Israel. When Babylon invaded Israel, they brought back many of the young people in order for them to live and work in Babylon.

Daniel, along with these three young men, were some of those chosen. Because of that extraction, they now had to live their lives and do their work in a worldly, idolatrous environment.

In fact, as they grew in wisdom and strength, they were handpicked to work for the federal government, as it were. They served as administrators in the regime of Nebuchadnezzar, who sat as the governing head of Babylon. They worked in a pagan-controlled place. This is not unlike many Christians today, who, due to circumstances in their lives, find themselves working in a pagan-controlled place. And while they are called to be lights that drive out the darkness and salt that preserves society, working in a secular space often presents challenges.

Shadrach, Meshach, and Abed-nego were about to learn that truth in real time. They were caught in a cultural tension. After all, how they had been raised in their Jewish faith contradicted with the worldview in which they now found themselves working. In fact, it conflicted so much that their very lives wound up at stake.

All of this started when Nebuchadnezzar developed his "theo-ego." He took on a god mentality. He deified himself. Desiring the worship of his subjects, he erected a statue of himself, which towered ninety feet high and nine feet wide. But the statue not only stood as a reminder to everyone of Nebuchadnezzar's self-prescribed god status; it also came to stand as a test for the three young Jewish men with regard to their loyalty and faith.

In Daniel 3:4–7, we read about how this test came about:

> Then the herald loudly proclaimed: "To you the command
> is given, O peoples, nations and men of every language, that

at the moment you hear the sound of the horn, flute, lyre, trigon, psaltery, bagpipe and all kinds of music, you are to fall down and worship the golden image that Nebuchadnezzar the king has set up. But whoever does not fall down and worship shall immediately be cast into the midst of a furnace of blazing fire." Therefore at that time, when all the peoples heard the sound of the horn, flute, lyre, trigon, psaltery, bagpipe and all kinds of music, all the peoples, nations and men of every language fell down and worshiped the golden image that Nebuchadnezzar the king had set up.

Forced worship had been set in place through this new law. As soon as any music was heard, people were required to fall down and worship the golden idol of Nebuchadnezzar. Like robots, they were to stop everything they were doing and direct their focus to the statue. Anyone who chose not to obey this command would have to pay the consequences for not compromising their personal values and beliefs.

The core issue at hand involved worship. Who were you going to worship? Similarly, throughout Scripture, the core issue of worship comes up time and again. At the heart of the Bible, from Genesis to Revelation, is this issue of idolatry. As we discussed in an earlier chapter, an idol is any noun—a person, place, thing, or thought—you look to as your source. Whether that is your source of safety, pleasure, provision, status, or any number of things is not the point. Whatever usurps God's rightful place in your life as your Source of all things becomes an idol. God is to be first, always (see Matt. 6:33).

These three young men would not, and could not, bow to

the idol if they were to keep God in His rightful place as Lord and King. So Shadrach, Meshach, and Abed-nego found themselves in a dilemma, and their career was on the line.

Yet while all of this was taking place, racism reared its ugly head, too. A racial challenge broke out because verse 8 tells us that these three young men became targets. We read, "For this reason at that time certain Chaldeans came forward and brought charges against the Jews." Bear in mind, the Babylonians didn't like the Jews. They didn't want the Jews working in their land because they were taking some of the highest esteemed jobs. Not only that but these Jews also brought their faith to work. They were known followers of the one, true God. But because they had done outstanding work, they couldn't be condemned for poor work. The only charges the Babylonians were able to level against them included their faith. They were unwilling to bow to the statue. Office politics took a whole new level when the three young men wouldn't bow. Now those who discriminated against them had a reason to bring charges on them, and it looked as if they would lose not only their jobs but also their lives.

When the king found out about their rebellion, he became enraged. He ordered that they be brought to him immediately. We read in verse 13, "Then Nebuchadnezzar in rage and anger gave orders to bring Shadrach, Meshach, and Abed-nego; then these men were brought before the king." Once the men were brought to him, he scolded them and gave them a second chance to bow to his command. Mocking them, he told them the results if their rebellion continued in, what he thought to be, a rhetorical question. Verse 15 says,

"Now if you are ready, at the moment you hear the sound of the horn, flute, lyre, trigon, psaltery and bagpipe and all kinds of music, to fall down and worship the image that I have made, very well. But if you do not worship, you will immediately be cast into the midst of a furnace of blazing fire; and what god is there who can deliver you out of my hands?"

The king believed that no one could overrule him. The king believed that no one had more power than he had. The king believed that no one could reverse something he put in motion. He felt that he was so strong and his nation so powerful and his government in so much control, that if he fired someone, they were fired. And I don't mean that in just the work-related sense of the term.

These men stared at an egomaniac who believed he held their fate in his hands. Now, that's a difficult situation to be in, to say the least. Their situation gives us insight into what God will allow when He wants to give us a kingdom encounter with Him. Because sometimes God will let you be put in a situation where you have to choose between two gods. Maybe it's the god of education, or your career. Or it could be the god of money that goes up against God. Whatever it is, God will allow you to be forced to choose.

Obviously, the king of Babylon had no idea that his rhetorical question wasn't very rhetorical at all. He had no idea as to the full scope and power of the true King. But the three men did. We know this because of their reply. We read in verses 16–18 the way these men chose to go:

"O Nebuchadnezzar, we do not need to give you an answer concerning this matter. If it be so, our God whom we serve is able to deliver us from the furnace of blazing fire; and He will deliver us out of your hand, O king. But even if He does not, let it be known to you, O king, that we are not going to serve your gods or worship the golden image that you have set up."

The men stand as a group to give their response, essentially telling the king that they don't need to give him an answer as to what they are going to do because he already knows what they are going to. They are going to refuse to bow, again. That point is already crystal clear. But to emphasize their point, they went a step further in their reply. They let the king know that the God whom they serve can deliver them. And even if He doesn't, they will never bow.

There's an interesting set of words that show up in their reply that, if we apply it to our own lives, will give us a greater opportunity for kingdom encounters. These words are "whom we serve." The men didn't just say their God would deliver them. No, they made it clear that the God whom they serve would deliver them. See, a lot of believers choose not to serve God but, at the same time, want a blessing from God. They want deliverance from God. They want an encounter with God. But if you take a look at their lives and actions, they look more like the surrounding culture than a reflection of God.

Scripture tells us clearly that wherever we are and whatever we are doing, we are to serve the Lord. When you go to work, you don't ultimately work for your boss. You work for the

Lord Christ whom you serve. Whether you are a paper-pusher, typist, teacher, lawyer, or any other worker, you are to carry out service to the Lord. As the apostle Paul exhorts, "Whether, then, you eat or drink or whatever you do, do all to the glory of God" (1 Cor. 10:31). "It is the Lord Christ whom you serve," in all things (Col. 3:24).

Believers love to quote Ephesians 3:20, especially when faced with a difficulty in life. You will often hear the phrase "He is able," or "My God is able." While God certainly is able, Ephesians 3:20 is not a blanket promise to anyone. This promise assumes something is working inside of you first. The entire verse reads like this: "Now to Him who is able to do far more abundantly beyond all that we ask or think, according to the power that works within us."

In order to tap into the "able" part of this promise, there needs to be a "power" at work within you. If the Spirit has no room to work within you, transforming you into the likeness of Jesus Christ in all you do and say (Rom. 8:29), then the deliverance isn't yours to simply claim. These three men in Babylon served God. They put their money where their mouth was. They didn't just go to church on Sunday. Rather, their entire lives— their thoughts, words, and actions—reflected internal hearts of service to God. Unfortunately today, many Christians divorce their everyday lives from their service to God—and then complain when God doesn't show up for them.

SERVING GOD—NO MATTER WHAT

The Hebrew men made it clear that the God they served could deliver them. But they also made it clear that they would not complain if He did not. Rather, they would continue to serve Him because they trusted in Him and honored Him as God.

You've heard the phrase, "God is good, all the time. All the time, God is good." It's a great phrase, and it's a true phrase. But when God does not come through for us or deliver us the way we hoped He would, we throw the phrase out the window. We question whether God is really good. We confuse His "good" with our definition of "good." The three men in Babylon did not. They knew that God is good, even if He chose not to deliver them from the fire.

There are things you and I need to remember about God. He is powerful. He is able. But He is also sovereign. He chooses what He does based on His overarching plan. A kingdom theology and a biblical worldview understands that God must have the option, in any situation, to choose what the right thing is to do. Even if you and I don't agree with it. When you can live with that level of faith and that level of trust, that's when you get a kingdom encounter like the one we are looking at in this chapter. God doesn't deliver everyone who calls on Him to do so. Hopefully you are seeing through this compilation of Scripture-based situations that there is a causation frequently tied to God's provision, power, and deliverance. And that causation often depends on what we do.

The courage found in these three men came from their belief that nothing negative could happen to them that didn't first pass through God's fingers to allow it. Knowing this truth and living by it is freeing. It means you do not have to play the company game. You don't need to bend to office politics. Because once you do, you are saying that the company is your source.

Or the boss is your source. You never have to compromise your faith when put in a position to do so. If God lets you go through the fire, you have to understand the only reason it happened is because He allowed it for a reason.

If you are serving the Lord and He lets things go south on you, He had to okay it first. God is sovereign. And if He allowed something in your life that you perceive to be negative, He did it on purpose. And the endgame of His purpose is always good. Until you understand, believe, and apply this kingdom truth to your life, you may miss your kingdom encounters.

LOOK FOR GOD

Sometimes things have to get worse before they get better. Which is exactly what happened to these three men when they stood up to the king by refusing to bow. Nebuchadnezzar was in a rage before they responded, but after they responded, he was filled with wrath. In fact, he was so filled with wrath that even his face was altered. We read,

> Then Nebuchadnezzar was filled with wrath, and his facial expression was altered toward Shadrach, Meshach and Abed-nego. He answered by giving orders to heat the furnace seven times more than it was usually heated. He commanded certain valiant warriors who were in his army to tie up Shadrach, Meshach and Abed-nego in order to cast them into the furnace of blazing fire. (vv. 19–20)

The furnace was already hot enough to burn them to death. But the king got so mad that these obstinate men resisted bowing to him, that he told his guards to heat it up seven times hotter. He intended to burn them to a crisp. In biblical times, seven was known as the number of completion. The king put his final stamp on their extermination. It might be like, in today's culture, if a boss were to fire you that he takes it a step further and tells you that he will not give you a recommendation either, if someone tries to hire you. It's more than just firing you. It's making sure he ruins your life and your career to completion. This scenario can apply to any number of situations. It doesn't have to be about work. It could be about relationships, connections, finances, and more.

When Satan seeks to take someone out for standing up in faith for God and for rejecting idolatry, he often wants to take them out completely. But what you and I need to keep in mind is that even though the furnace might be turned up seven times hotter in attempt to ruin us, God sits outside of the physics on this earth. He is not bound to play by the rules of His creation. When the three men got tossed into the furnace, which burned hot enough to even kill those who were throwing them in (v. 22), the men themselves walked out unshackled and unharmed. Not only were they unharmed from the attack on their lives but they also didn't have to go through the process alone. When the king looked into the furnace to admire his demonically inspired handiwork of death, he got a huge surprise. The men were still alive. And instead of three of them, there were now four. We read about this in verses 24–25:

> "Was it not three men we cast bound into the midst of the fire?" They replied to the king, "Certainly, O king." He said, "Look! I see four men loosed and walking about in the midst of the fire without harm, and the appearance of the fourth is like a son of the gods!"

The king couldn't figure this out. He knew they put in three men. He asked the others if they also knew that they put in only three men. And last he checked, three still equaled three. But now, all of a sudden, there were four men in the furnace, and all of them were doing just fine. Nobody got burned. Nobody got harmed. Nobody got defeated as planned. They still went through the fire, yes. But while in the fire, God met them and kept them from harm.

Sometimes God will deliver you from whatever seeks to harm you. But there are other times when He wants to give you a special, unique encounter with Himself, so He chooses not to deliver you—and He joins you in the harm. Sometimes He wants you to see what it is like when you are in the fire, but like the bush Moses experienced, you are not burned up. Sometimes heaven wants to join you in a bad situation without taking you out of it. But whether He takes you from it or joins you in it, you have an encounter with the Living God because He has a perfect plan for it. So rather than getting all shook up when the devil has you tied up, open your eyes instead. Look for the presence of the living God and His calming peace for you. Fire doesn't have the last say when God is involved.

First Peter 2:20 tells us why God sometimes allows the fire in our lives: "For what credit is there if, when you sin and are harshly treated, you endure it with patience? But if when you do what is right and suffer for it you patiently endure it, this finds favor with God." When you do the right thing in the face of persecution, threat, pain, or any number of potential fears, you receive favor with God. Not only that, it also brings you His blessing.

Peter also says, "But even if you should suffer for the sake of righteousness, you are blessed. And do not fear their intimidation, and do not be troubled" (3:14). Do not be scared or troubled at what anyone threatens concerning you. It doesn't matter what their title is. It doesn't matter the authority they hold. No one holds more authority than the living God. He alone guards you. The following verses in 1 Peter 3 tell us more:

> But sanctify Christ as Lord in your hearts, always be-
> ing ready to make a defense to everyone who asks you to
> give an account for the hope that is in you, yet with gentle-
> ness and reverence; and keep a good conscience so that in
> the thing in which you are slandered, those who revile your
> good behavior in Christ will be put to shame. For it is bet-
> ter, if God should will it so, that you suffer for doing what is
> right rather than for doing what is wrong. (vv. 15–17)

We are to sanctify Christ as Lord in our hearts. That means to follow Him as Lord in every area of our lives. When we do, those who seek our demise will be "put to shame." Not only that, but 1 Peter 5:10 tells us that God will use the fires and trials of life brought by obedience to Him to perfect, confirm, strengthen, and establish us as His, under His rule and dominion. God's grace heals. God's grace protects. God's grace reverses. God's grace lifts up. God's grace even promotes.

Psalm 75:6–7 says, "For not from the east, nor from the west, nor from the desert comes exaltation; but God is the Judge; He puts down one and exalts another." Promotion comes from the Lord. Heaven decides when it's time for you to be promoted. And keep in mind, when Heaven decides it is time for you to be promoted, it doesn't matter who on earth doesn't want you to be promoted.

I worked at Trailways Bus during seminary. I was loading and unloading buses on the night shift while going to school during the day, in order to provide for my family. Not too long into the job, I was approached about a scheme going on where workers would trade off having someone else clock them in and then go off to take a nap. They wanted to know what time slot I wanted for my nap. That's when I looked at them and shook my head no, letting them know loud and clear that I didn't operate that way.

They took me aside and explained that it was just the way things were. But I explained I was a Christian and that was stealing. I let them know not only would I not steal from the company, but I would not help someone else steal from the company either.

Well, as you can imagine, no one liked my answer. So over the course of the next few months, they made my work life a living hell. Rather than helping me load or unload buses, they left me to do it all on my own. If they did help, they would leave the extra heavy boxes for me to do on my own. I wound up being severely tested and tried for my stand. This made me feel depressed and frustrated because I needed to provide for my family, and I needed the job. But the job was taking its physical toll on me. I admit I got the same attitude many of us get when things go south. I wondered why God allowed all of that difficulty to happen to me when I had stood up for what I believed He wanted me to do. I was faithful to Him, and He let me experience a very difficult scenario as a result.

A number of months into this ordeal, I got a call from the manager. I went into his office, and he informed me that they were aware of the scheme. He said they had put a night supervisor on board to observe, without anyone else knowing, what was going on. He said they were also aware that I had not participated in the scheme. So what they did was promote me! They made me a manager on the night shift.

Now, I didn't know someone else was watching. I just did what was right because I knew it was right. But God had put a fourth person in the fire with me in order for them to promote me as a result of my obedience to Him. You have to understand that when God decides to promote you, it doesn't matter what humanity says.

Look at what the king did with the three men once he realized they had been delivered in the midst of his own fire. Daniel 3 concludes:

> Nebuchadnezzar responded and said, "Blessed be the God of Shadrach, Meshach and Abed-nego, who has sent His angel and delivered His servants who put their trust in Him, violating the king's command, and yielded up their bodies so as not to serve or worship any god except their

own God. Therefore I make a decree that any people, nation or tongue that speaks anything offensive against the God of Shadrach, Meshach and Abed-nego shall be torn limb from limb and their houses reduced to a rubbish heap, inasmuch as there is no other god who is able to deliver in this way." Then the king caused Shadrach, Meshach and Abed-nego to prosper in the province of Babylon. (vv. 28–30)

The king, the one who had sent them to their deaths, caused them to prosper. The truth within that statement is that the one, true King caused the king of Babylon to make them prosper. The hearts of kings are turned to and fro by the power of God Himself (Prov. 21:1). Trust Him. Your circumstances may look scary to you right now. You may be under spiritual or human attack. But keep your eyes focused on God; serve Him daily with your thoughts, words, and actions; and when necessary, draw a line in the sand. He has a plan for you. It is a good plan. He knows how long He will allow the fire. He knows you have bills to pay. He knows how to reverse the health issue. He can do it all. What you need to do in the midst of the trial is stay faithful to Him and keep your eyes open for His kingdom encounter with you. Take your stand for God. He rules over all.

CHAPTER 7

Encountering God's Process

A seed has to break before a plant comes from it. Water must break before a baby emerges. A stallion must be broken before the rider can control it. The seal of cologne or perfume must be cracked before the aroma emerges. The shell of a peanut must be opened before the nut can be enjoyed. In other words, to get to the core of a thing, its benefit, a breaking must occur.

In order for you to have a kingdom encounter with the living God, you too must be broken. Without brokenness, the experience of God in which you get to see Him with your own eyes and His reality becomes alive for you will evade you.

The reason many of us are still waiting on our breakthrough is because we've not yet been broken. We have not yet been to the place where God has been free to express Himself to us, for us, and through us because we remain unbroken. Psalm 138:6 helps us to see this truth through the unfolding of these words,

"For though the LORD is exalted, yet He regards the lowly, but the haughty He knows from afar." Far too many believers have a long-distance relationship with God rather than an up-close experience of Him because they insist on not being broken. Yet brokenness (lowliness) is a criterion of a kingdom encounter. When that doesn't take place, God remains to you a theology on the shelf or a concept and idea without being the dynamic reality that He truly is.

To be broken spiritually means to be stripped of your self-sufficiency. It means God has ripped you of your independence. It is when you come to the place where you discover the truth of the statement found in John 15:5: "apart from Me you can do nothing." As long as you live independently of God with a self-sufficient mindset, you remain unbroken. And as long as you remain unbroken, you remain unchanged. As a result, your encounter with God escapes you.

To encounter God's presence involves embracing His process of stripping you of your self-reliance so that you can experience a new level of His reality in your life. God keeps His distance from prideful, unbroken people (Ps. 138:6).

MORE THAN YOU CAN BEAR

Before we go further, it's important for me to debunk a myth in Christianity that you may have heard or may even believe. Nearly every Christian has quoted it at least once in their lives or had it quoted to them. But unfortunately, it's not truth. And when we live our lives according to a lie, we will experience pain, emptiness, and a continual gap in our encounters with God. The myth is this: God will not put on you more than you can bear.

Yes, that may sound good. It may even sound like it's in the Bible somewhere. It definitely can make you feel good. It's just not true. There are times in our lives when God will put more on us than we can bear on our own. The reason why He does is that He wants to break you. Paul writes about the time when he suffered from hopeless thoughts and a desire to give up altogether. This is the great apostle Paul. This is the Paul who penned a large portion of the entire New Testament. Yes, he struggled. He suffered. He felt like throwing in the towel. I mentioned it briefly in another chapter but want to reinforce its importance here because Paul tells us why God puts more on than we can bear in 2 Corinthians 1:8–10. He shares,

> For we do not want you to be unaware, brethren, of our affliction which came to us in Asia, that we were burdened excessively, beyond our strength, so that we despaired even of life; indeed, we had the sentence of death within ourselves so that we would not trust in ourselves, but in God who raises the dead; who delivered us from so great a peril of death, and will deliver us, He on whom we have set our hope. And He will yet deliver us.

Paul speaks openly of his struggles in this passage. These weren't only his struggles, either. He spoke of the struggles of the group of people with him at that time. They wanted to quit. They felt overwhelmed. They couldn't take it anymore. But after speaking openly on these truths, Paul explained why God allowed it. God allowed the affliction so that they might experience and encounter Him more fully. God wanted them to know He is the One who delivered them, delivers them, and will deliver them. This was also God's motivation in not answering Paul's request for deliverance from the messenger of Satan that was attacking him. God was allowing the attack to take the apostle deeper in his experience of God's power and grace (2 Cor. 12:7–9).

Sometimes God will let you be put in a death-grip where you feel so burdened with pain and problems that the temptation you face is one of giving up. You just feel like you can't make it another day. When God puts you in that situation, He is trying to break you for the purposes of remaking you. Brokenness is when God intervenes in your life through a negative set of circumstances in order to attack (and consequently seek to cure) a flaw in your humanity. There exists a flaw in your personhood that desperately needs to be addressed. In fact, there exist many flaws. But one of the main flaws we all face is rooted in our core. It is the false spirit of independence and self-sufficiency. In order for us to grow and develop into who we are destined to be, God must strip us of this basic flaw. And He does that through a process of breaking us.

Why We Are Broken

Let's look at this concept deeper by examining who you are as described in Scripture. First Thessalonians 5:23 tells us, "Now may the God of peace Himself sanctify you entirely; and may your spirit and soul and body be preserved complete, without blame at the coming of our Lord Jesus Christ." This passage directly states that we are made up of three things: spirit, soul, and body. Your body allows you to function in the physical world through your five senses. You relate to the world around you and exist on the earth through this body. Your soul is your personhood and self-identity. The soul is that life principle that allows the body to operate. Lastly, your spirit is your direct connection with God.

Everyone who is born into the world is born here with a scarred soul. Sin has scarred our souls. We have been born in sin, shaped in iniquity. Thus, we have flaws. This shows up at different levels for different people but there exists a scarring of the soul in all of us. This scarring only increases over time as negative things happen to us, circumstances overwhelm us, wrong is done to us, or sin is done by us. All of this adds up to additional scarring of our souls. This scarring of the soul breeds independence from God.

Yet when a person accepts salvation through faith alone in Christ alone, the Holy Spirit invades their human spirit thereby giving them the ability to now receive new spiritual data. As the Holy Spirit enters the human spirit, He also enters a portal to the soul, enabling the soul's transformation as well as the healing of the scars. This healing takes place on many levels and in many ways. Some of those ways involve stripping us of our self-sufficiency and removing the build-up of our ego that has accumulated in our soul. If this build-up is allowed to remain and corrode our conscience, we then do wrong things with our bodies. That's why it is so important for the Spirit to heal us in order that we might function in the full measure and capacity that will bring God glory and spread good to those around us, as well as to ourselves.

This internal transformation is designed to usher in a change in the life and character of the person. But in order to heal the soul, God must break it first so that He can penetrate it. He must invade it by entering it in order to dominate it. Of course, our souls naturally resist that invasion. Our souls do not want to be invaded by this divine interruption to our plans, desires, and dreams. So, more often than not, we resist His invasion. This then causes God to have to go deeper in the penetration and the breaking. Unfortunately, the longer it takes you to break only increases the level of breaking you need in order for God to strip you down. God can't give you a kingdom encounter with Him as long as you are self-reliant. He must break you to re-build you.

In Genesis 32, we see this kind of breaking in the life of the patriarch Jacob. If you don't know much about the life of Jacob, his name can give you insight. In the Bible, names carried significance and meaning. They were given in order to explain the character of the person. Jacob's name meant "supplanter, trickster, or deceiver." He was a born deceiver. From the time he left his mother's womb, he set out to get that which was not his own. He was known as the "heel grabber" for coming out of the womb with his hand on his brother's heel. Genesis 25:26 (NIV) says, "After this, his brother came out, with his hand grasping Esau's heel; so he was named Jacob." Later, Jacob would go on to trick his brother, Esau, out of his birthright. Obviously, Jacob lived up to his name. He would do whatever it took to get one over on the next person. That was his M.O. That wasn't a one-time thing or a mistake. No, deception and trickery were a lifestyle for Jacob.

Which is exactly why God needed to break him. It's important to note that God will often use people or circumstances to break a person, just like He did with Jacob. As you can imagine, his brother, Esau, was not happy about how Jacob had tricked him out of his birthright. In fact, Esau was so enraged that he wanted to kill Jacob. We gain insight into this situation by looking at Genesis 32:6–8:

> The messengers returned to Jacob, saying, "We came to your brother Esau, and furthermore he is coming to meet you, and four hundred men are with him." Then Jacob was greatly afraid and distressed; and he divided the people who were with him, and the flocks and the herds and the camels, into two companies; for he said, "If Esau comes to the one company and attacks it, then the company which is left will escape."

Esau had rounded up a small army of four hundred men in order to annihilate his brother, Jacob, and all Jacob owned. To avoid complete destruction, Jacob chose the strategy of intentional division. He broke his herds and groups into two. That way when Esau attacked one, the other could still flee. Jacob's trickery had finally caught up with him and was about to overtake him. But as we see in the next few verses, Jacob's fear caused him to do something wise. He called out to God. He prayed,

> "O God of my father Abraham and God of my father Isaac, O LORD, who said to me, 'Return to your country and to your relatives, and I will prosper you,' I am unworthy of

all the lovingkindness and of all the faithfulness which You have shown to Your servant; for with my staff only I crossed this Jordan, and now I have become two companies. Deliver me, I pray, from the hand of my brother, from the hand of Esau; for I fear him, that he will come and attack me and the mothers with the children. For You said, 'I will surely prosper you and make your descendants as the sand of the sea, which is too great to be numbered.'" (vv. 9–12)

Jacob was scared. His life was on the line. His family's lives were on the line. As was his legacy. What's worse was that it was all his fault. His trickery and deception had caught up with him, leaving him in a space of despondency. He didn't think he could, or would, make it on his own. Sound familiar? Have you ever been a position where you did not feel you could make it on your own? We all have at some point in our lives. But what you need to remember when you are in one is that God allows these situations for a reason.

When God puts you in something you cannot change, fix, repair, get out of, or alter yourself, it's because He has begun the process of breaking you in order to remake you. Jacob's back was up against the wall. He was desperate, crying out to God. His brother and four hundred men were charging toward him and all that he loved. He was scared. So he asked for God's help.

HELP UNLIKE WHAT WE EXPECT

God did send Jacob help, but it did not come in the way anyone would expect—as is often the case when God intervenes. We read about God's help in verse 24: "Then Jacob was left alone, and a man wrestled with him until daybreak." For starters, Jacob was alone. It was night. He was scared. He was worried about his family. He was concerned for his life. He had called out to God. And as a result, he got attacked. Out of nowhere in the dark of the night, God sent someone to grab him. Things went from bad to worse.

Does it ever feel like things go from bad to worse when you pray to God? Sometimes you wonder why you even prayed. But God has a reason for the wrestling He allows in your life, as we'll see with Jacob's story. Jacob is now in the fight of his life. What's more is that this fight won't seem to end. As we saw in verse 24, he wrestled with him all night long. To say that Jacob put up a fight is an understatement. He hung in there. He didn't give up. He kept wrestling with this stranger throughout the early hours of the morning.

Yet when the man saw that Jacob wouldn't give up, he did something more. He gave Jacob a disadvantage. Scripture says, "He touched the socket of his thigh; so the socket of Jacob's thigh was dislocated while he wrestled with him" (Gen 32:25). If you follow or watch wrestling, you know that the goal is to bring your opponent into submission. This other person was seeking to get Jacob to submit, so he dislocated his hip socket to bring this about quicker. The hip socket is part of the core of your body. When someone is weight training for a sport, they are seeking to build up their core. The reason for this is because that's where their strength and power comes from. So the fastest way to reduce Jacob's strength in this wrestling match was to dislocate his core. He disconnected him at the point of his power. In other words, Jacob put up such a lengthy fight that his opponent knew he was still relying on his own strength. He was still getting by on what he could muster. He hadn't been broken yet. As such, he wasn't getting the point.

Thus, God had to make it worse. See, when God is trying to break you, He will make it bad. But if you are still not responding to what He is doing, and you are still relying on your own ways, He will make it worse. He will take you even lower and lower until you get the message.

Jacob got the message when his hip socket broke. He couldn't go on. On top of that, he saw that his opponent broke his socket with a simple touch of his finger. Obviously, if his opponent can dislocate his socket just by touching it with his finger, he was capable of a lot more. It wasn't a fair fight after all. But Jacob also learned that the opponent wasn't out to kill him. Because if he could dislocate his hip by touching it with his finger, you can imagine what he could do with his heart. The fight would be over right then and there. This principle is important for us to realize because there are times when God is pursuing the process of breaking us that it feels like we can't go on. As Paul said earlier, you can get to the point where you despair even of life itself. But what you have to remember in those times is that God is not trying to overpower you entirely. Rather, He is trying to break you at your core so that you will no longer depend on yourself but will look to Him instead. Brokenness is often the only way to experiencing a kingdom encounter with the living God.

At daybreak, Jacob came to realize something he couldn't

see at night. God was in the struggle. He finally got the message, after he had been stripped of his own sufficiency and self-worth. He finally understood the true power of the one with whom he wrestled. Jacob realized that he was not wrestling another human being. It was a man, yes, but he wasn't human. Not with the strength and power he had. Upon realizing this, Jacob knew that this was not merely a physical battle. This was a spiritual battle. That's when he chose to do the right thing. He chose to do what we all should do when we are broken in the physical realm. Realizing that a greater spiritual war was taking place, Jacob appealed for a spiritual result. Jacob asked for a blessing. He refused to let this stranger go until he blessed him (v. 26). Jacob decided to hang on until he heard from God.

GOD HONORS TRANSPARENCY

The stranger's response might surprise you. Instead of conferring a blessing, he asked him his name. Now, remember what we looked at earlier in the chapter? A name refers to a person's character. Jacob was a trickster and a deceiver. The opponent was asking Jacob to reveal who he was to him. He wanted to see whether he was willing to admit it. He wanted to force Jacob to acknowledge who he truly was and how he had truly behaved throughout his life. Jacob was a deeply flawed human being. He used evil to get by. He misused people. But before his blessing would come, he had to be honest about this. He had to admit he was a liar. Why? Because God is not interested in what is fake. Matthew 5:8 puts it this way, "Blessed are the pure in heart, for they shall see God."

We have so much fake going on in our culture today. Fake jewelry. Fake identities. Fake personalities. Fake histories. Fake friends. Fake contacts. Fake news. Fake images. Fake brands. We live in a Jacob society, full of deception. That means that few of us are having any meaningful encounters with God because the reverse of Matthew 5:8 is true as well: the impure in heart (the fake) will not see God. Transparency with God is a prerequisite to a kingdom encounter.

So many Christians today cry out to God for a blessing, but God wants to know how bad they really want it. Jacob didn't get his blessing until he came clean with God. You and I must be willing to face our nature. We must be willing to live authentically before God. At the center of having a pure heart lies honesty. If we can't be honest with God, we can't have the kingdom encounters with God that transform our lives.

Jacob answered his opponent quickly. He told him his name. Then the man he wrestled with all night changed Jacob's name. He said, "'Your name shall no longer be Jacob, but Israel; for you have striven with God and with men and have prevailed'" (v. 28). Jacob got a name change. He got a new identity. His name would stand as a constant reminder of who owned him. In biblical times, naming something signified owning it. By naming Jacob "Israel," which means "God helps or God fights," God let him know that He owned him. His old name reflected a life of self-reliance. His new name recognized that God Himself is his sufficiency. He was to depend on the divine.

In changing his name, God let Jacob know that He had a new reality for him to experience. He was not to live a life of trickery anymore. He was not to deceive anymore. He wasn't to try to fix it himself through his own ways. Instead, God would exercise His ownership in Israel's life.

Some of us could use a name change as well. Maybe we have a name tied to our education. Or we have a name tied to our history. Some of us have a name tied to our relationships. Whatever the case, unless your character is rooted in God's sufficiency alone, He will have to change your name. And He will often do that by allowing the things or people you used to rely on to fail so that you will learn that the spiritual trumps the physical. Neither you nor I are sufficient within ourselves. Until we learn this and are willing to let go of our own securities, we will never experience God as we ought to. Difficulties teach dependence. David speaks of that like this: "It is good for me that I was afflicted, that I may learn Your statutes" (Ps. 119:71).

Friend, God may bring you down in order to lift you up. So when God puts you in a situation that is outside of your control, where you feel isolated and afraid, seeing no human solution, understand that He is using the physical elements and environment to break through on something spiritual. Don't mistake the hand of God for the hand of man.

Jacob realized this truth and received his new name: Israel. Then he asked the man with whom he wrestled what his name was as well. Scripture doesn't say that the man laughed at the question, but I imagine he might have because his answer sounds like he did: "Why is it that you ask My name?" In other words, "I just wrestled with you all night. I dislocated your hip with the tip of my finger. You asked me to bless you. And I gave you a new name. If my name isn't clear to you by now, then my telling you it isn't going to change your understanding." Basically, he wanted Jacob to put two and two together on his own. It wasn't that deep! He ought to have known whom he was dealing with by then! Then, instead of giving Jacob his name, he blessed him there (v. 29).

Even though the man did not answer, Jacob found out he already knew His name. We know this because of what he named the place. Verse 30 says, "So Jacob named the place Peniel, for he said, 'I have seen God face to face, yet my life has been preserved.'" Jacob knew he could have lost his life that night. But because of the goodness and grace of God, he was spared. He knew who his opponent was. He also knew how fortunate he had been to encounter Him and still live to tell about it. He had gotten his blessing, a change of name that re-established his covenantal legacy. But by the name he gave the place, we can see that he had received the humility he needed as well. The name didn't refer to his blessing. It didn't refer to what he did in wrestling all night long. The name he gave the place referenced the sparing of his life by the Almighty God who has power over all.

As Jacob left the place of his transformation, he left with a souvenir as well. He left with a reminder. He left with a battle scar, which he would cherish for the rest of his life. He left with a legacy. Verses 31–32 say,

> Now the sun rose upon him just as he crossed over Penuel, and he was limping on his thigh. Therefore, to this day the sons of Israel do not eat the sinew of the hip which is

on the socket of the thigh, because he touched the socket of Jacob's thigh in the sinew of the hip.

He left with a limp. This limp would serve as a perpetual reminder of his blessing. It would serve as an ongoing testimony of his name change and transformation. This limp was his badge of honor. We know that he kept it throughout his life because in Hebrews 11:21 it says, "By faith Jacob, as he was dying, blessed each of the sons of Joseph, and worshiped, leaning on the top of his staff." Even years later, he was limping. He leaned on a staff to walk. But that limp wasn't a negative reminder. That limp spoke of a kingdom encounter with a massive impact. It spoke of a person who used to be independent, self-sufficient, and deceptive. But it also spoke to the power of God to transform that person into a dependent, devoted, and honest servant of the Most High God. Every step Jacob took reminded him that he can't make it without God. Every limp warned him never to get the "big head" again or think too highly of himself. His blessing came tied to his humility, and his humility was rooted in his brokenness.

I doubt that Jacob minded his limp. He probably enjoyed it. Because that limp got him to the point of surrender so that he could receive the blessing.

A blessing is often something God had planned to do in the past for you but is not free to do yet. There are many reasons why He's not free to act on the blessing, yet one of them is our pride. Pride will always stand between you and your blessing. Pride will block your kingdom encounter. But if you really want to experience God up close and personal, you need to seek His process. You have to be willing to be broken so that you can be truly and totally dependent upon Him.

Maybe when you were growing up, you had a piggy bank. There would always be a slit on the top of piggy banks. The slit is where you would put in your coins or paper money. When it was time to take the money out, you would shake your piggy bank. Turning it upside down, you would shake it and shake it until the money fell out. The reason you shook it so hard was because there was something valuable on the inside that you wanted to come out. The harder you shook, the more it would come out. You weren't hating on the piggy bank. You weren't mad at the piggy bank. You just wanted what was inside the piggy bank to come out. In fact, sometimes some of you might have gotten a hammer to smash the piggy bank in order to get the money out!

God will shake us to bring out the spiritual treasures that His Holy Spirit has implanted in us to come out. He will allow things to get unsteady or situations to become challenging. But if you or I won't respond to the shaking at the level He desires, He may have to break us as well. The question is do you want to have to wrestle all night long only to have your hip dislocated before you will surrender? Or will you come before the living Lord and surrender to Him right now? Lay your will at His feet. Let your control be relinquished into His control. Honor His will above your own desires. When you do, you will encounter His love, purpose, and blessings in a powerful way. Remember, brokenness is pain with a purpose.

CHAPTER 8

Encountering God's Petition

On October 24, 1929, the stock market crashed. This gave way to what become known as the Great Depression. People lost their life savings. Homes were foreclosed. People were laid off from work by the droves due to this new economic reality. Our nation faced a national depression that had ripple effects reaching worldwide.

But for many of us, we don't need October 24, 1929, to teach us what it means to be depressed. Far too many today understand depression all too well. Lives are collapsing all around us as person after person gives in to anxiety, despair, and doubt. Great pain has become normative for our culture. Fear has replaced calm.

The kingdom encounter that so many of us need has nothing to do with our circumstances. It has to do with the ability to remain in our right minds. Because circumstances will change. Food will be in abundance one day and scarce the next. Health can be present one day and absent the next. Security may appear to rule one day and chaos the next. Yet it's in the ability to remain mentally strong, at peace internally, that will carry you through.

The great prophet Elijah lived a life of extreme circumstances. He experienced divine interventions and miracles unlike that which most of us ever will. But the miracle I want us to look at in this chapter has nothing to do with the material world. This miracle had everything to do with Elijah's need to be lifted out of his depression.

Now, depression is not discouragement. Discouragement is often a result of some sort of loss. A person may get discouraged if they lost their job, health, or a relationship. This can usher in a fog or an overcast sky in the mind of this person. This is normal. But when discouragement continues and elongates itself, it devolves into depression. Depression is discouragement on steroids. It is discouragement that has now produced an ongoing level of gloom, emotional pain, and even despair. When depression becomes despair, it can produce a sense of hopelessness. You see no way out. You see no "exit" sign. There's no way to get around this thing. You can't find the path to beat it or escape it. It simply will not go away.

When a person's discouragement results in depression and that depression is allowed to linger, they may wind up considering the possibility of death.

All of us have felt discouragement at some point in our lives. Some of us have even felt despair. And there are those who have also considered suicide. This is why Elijah's kingdom encounter ought to speak to everyone reading this book. Because if you and I can just discover how to get our minds thinking right, no matter what happens externally, we will be okay. You are in control of your thoughts. You choose what you allow to linger and what you choose to cast down. That's what we see in the life of Elijah.

TAKING CONTROL OF YOUR MIND

In this particular situation in Elijah's life, he's on the run. He's taken off at lightning speed because the hand of the Lord was upon him. He had just destroyed the four hundred prophets of Ba'al in an act of mighty faith. He had to have been feeling good when that happened. But immediately his situation changed. His world collapsed, and his life became in jeopardy, which took him from the mountaintop of victory deep down into the valley of despair. He has found himself where many of us find ourselves: in a black hole. He's looking for the light at the end of the tunnel even though it appears to only be the light of an on-coming train. His whole world got turned upside down in a day.

We read about this in 1 Kings 19:1–5:

> Now Ahab told Jezebel everything Elijah had done and how he had killed all the prophets with the sword. So Je-zebel sent a messenger to Elijah to say, "May the gods deal with me, be it ever so severely, if by this time tomorrow I do not make your life like that of one of them." Elijah was afraid and ran for his life. When he came to Beersheba in Judah, he left his servant there, while he himself went a

day's journey into the wilderness. He came to a broom bush, sat down under it and prayed that he might die. "I have had enough, LORD," he said. "Take my life; I am no better than my ancestors." Then he lay down under the bush and fell asleep. (NIV)

As you can see, Jezebel was running this show. Jezebel was calling the shots. And Jezebel wanted Elijah's head on a platter. She wanted him dead.

You may not have a literal "Jezebel" in your life. But Jezebel can be considered as any evil threat that comes your way. It is something, or someone, who threatens the stability of your mental well-being. When a boss threatens you or a person irritates your personal stability, they are being a Jezebel in your life. They are operating as the new ruler over your emotions. And the reason why they can operate over you like that is because when their threat gets in your head and in your thoughts, it affects your feelings.

Now, since your emotions are part of your soul, how your soul relates to your thoughts can help you understand how to find the way to deal with harmful emotions. Your emotions are like the caboose on a train. Your mind is like the engine. When the engine of a train goes up the mountain, the caboose is going to go with it because the caboose is hooked on to the engine. When the engine goes down into the valley, the caboose is going to go with it because the caboose is going to follow wherever the engine winds up. Thus, if your mind is wrong, then your emotions are going to be wrong. If your mind is right, then your emotions are going to be right.

That's why changing your mind will always change how you feel.

For example, if you were struggling emotionally due to financial setbacks, and I just told you that I was going to give you a million dollars, how would you feel? I can tell you that no matter how bad you felt before I told you that, you would feel the opposite of that once you heard the news. In fact, you might just start running around, jumping, shouting, flipping, and celebrating because you got new information in the engine that affected the caboose.

You must understand that your emotions are the caboose. They are real. But they are not always true. Because they follow the engine of your thought, they can be swayed. Thus, if a Jezebel is allowed to get into your mind, it can then control your emotions. One reason so many of us have feelings that are out of control is because a Jezebel has gotten into our mind and has taken control. But the truth is *you* have control over whether or not she stays there.

In the Scripture we just read, Elijah was giving into the threat. He was allowing Jezebel to steal his mental energy and thus his will to even live. He went from hero prophet to man on the run overnight simply because he let someone else get into his thoughts. We find him sitting underneath a juniper tree, asking God to take his life.

Seeing how fast he fell from the pinnacle to the pit is amazing. Only twenty-four hours earlier, he was celebrating the victory of defeating Ba'al. Now, he was in despair. That is a very fast slippery slope. But remember, Elijah is not an unspiritual person.

He has been called a man of God. We read in 1 Kings 18:45–46 that God was with him:

> Meanwhile, the sky grew black with clouds, the wind rose, a heavy rain started falling and Ahab rode off to Jezreel. The power of the LORD came on Elijah and, tucking his cloak into his belt, he ran ahead of Ahab all the way to Jezreel. (NIV)

Guess what? It is possible for spiritual people to get depressed. Depression is not a sign of a lack of spirituality. We are human. In our flesh and blood, we become subject to influences that trigger thoughts in our minds. So never give in to the thought that spiritual people do not become down. Paul despaired of his life. Elijah despaired of his life. Spiritual people get depressed. Moses did. Job did. David did. In fact, David was depressed a lot. In the Psalms, we read how he goes from one mountain to a valley time and time again. We read several times where he asks himself, "Soul, why are you so downcast?" He talks to himself because he is trying to talk himself out of his own depression (read Ps. 42).

BE HONEST WITH GOD

Denying depression is worse than acknowledging it. Because in acknowledging the authenticity of who you are in that moment in time, you are being real. You are positioning yourself to address it in order to overcome it. Elijah didn't tell God that he was fine. He didn't say that he was tired and just needed to sleep it off. No, Elijah made it clear that he had had enough. He asked God to take his life so he could be done with the fight.

But God had a different plan in mind. He had a different way of dealing with Elijah's depression. We read about this in verses 5–6:

> Then he lay down under the bush and fell asleep. All at once an angel touched him and said, "Get up and eat." He looked around, and there by his head was some bread baked over hot coals, and a jar of water. He ate and drank and then lay down again. (NIV)

Elijah had fallen asleep but he was awakened by an angel. The angel touched him and gave him a cake. You could say this is the first introduction of angel-food cake. And since the angel fed Elijah, we know that this was not normal food. This was supernatural food. It contained within it the ability to restore him.

I want you to notice, though, *when* the angel showed up. The angel showed up after Elijah was honest with his emotions. The angel appeared after Elijah spoke truthfully with God. He had told God that he wanted to die. He had told God that he was not as good as his ancestors. He admitted who he was and what he lacked. Then God met his need.

The reason why many of us don't get what we need is because we are not honest with God. We play church. We play religion. We certainly play prayer. We get all spiritual and sophisticated with our words. But God doesn't care about how sophisticated we sound. He cares how honest we are. Elijah got raw with God. Elijah knew how he felt, and he admitted it. His honesty opened the door for a supernatural kingdom encounter.

Elijah was certainly disappointed in himself at this point. It's possible that he was even disappointed with God. Whatever the case, he was honest. He spoke a truth-telling prayer. He knew he was being chased by a powerful enemy. He knew he didn't have much hope, if any at all. When you are that low, there is no time for cute-sounding prayers. There is no time to play church or participate in rote religious activity. It is time to get raw with God.

TAKE CARE OF YOUR BODY

I want you to notice how God chose to address Elijah. He sent an angel to provide for his physical need of food. He took care of the body. He gave him a cake and then some water. After which, He told him to rest. The point being that proper care of our physical bodies impacts our spiritual and psychological health as well. If you are physically "off," then you will be off in other ways as well. God sought to restore Elijah's body before moving on to anything else.

When we get drained in our physical form, it will negatively impact everything else.

One of my highest points of the week is when I preach on Sunday morning. It's similar to a mountain-top experience for me. I get so excited to preach that I jump out of bed at five in the morning every Sunday. I cannot wait to get to church and preach for two services, as well as to experience the collective worship of the church body.

But one of my lowest points comes around 1:30 on Sunday afternoon, after I have greeted the last guest and then get in my car to drive home. Even as I walk to the car, I can feel the energy draining out of me. I can feel it leaving. It dissipates. All I want to do is go sit down for a while. This may be due to the sheer amount of physical, emotional, and spiritual exertion that takes place as I preach. But whatever the case, there is not a whole lot left in me afterwards. The human body can take only so much.

Elijah was human. He had a nature like ours (James 5:17). His suicidal thoughts may have become exacerbated due to the reality of his physical, emotional, and spiritual exhaustion. Those are the times when the enemy seeks to throw us off base. The enemy seeks to trip us up. In fact, when the devil tempted Jesus in the desert, Jesus was hungry, tired, and emotionally isolated. When we let our bodies go—or fail to properly care for our physical needs—we open ourselves up for attack. That's why rest is so important. That's why eating well is so important. Neglecting our physical needs damages all else. There is a domino effect.

Don't Play the Victim

Thankfully, God can meet us in our times of testing and trials. He can send us angels, as He did with Elijah, to restore our physical bodies. And when He does, He not only meets your physical needs but He also guides and directs you. After Elijah had eaten the cake, drank the water, and rested, the angel touched him again and gave him some instructions. We read,

> The angel of the LORD came back a second time and touched him and said, "Get up and eat, for the journey is too much for you." So he got up and ate and drank.

Strengthened by that food, he traveled forty days and forty nights until he reached Horeb, the mountain of God. There he went into a cave and spent the night. (1 Kings 19:7–9 NIV)

One way you can identify a kingdom encounter is when you are given strength beyond what should be normal. The angel of the Lord gave Elijah something else to eat, and this food gave him enough strength to travel for forty days and forty nights until he would reach the presence of God. The mountain of God was symbolically named for the presence of God. The angel knew that if Elijah's emotions were to be restored, he would need to enter into the presence of God.

Once Elijah reached the presence of God, he heard the voice of the Lord ask him why he had come. It's not that God Himself needed to know that answer. Sometimes questions are asked in order to give the person the opportunity to verbalize the answer for themselves. Elijah did just that. He responded to the question as to why he was there by sharing the hurt and betrayal within his heart:

> "I have been very zealous for the LORD God Almighty. The Israelites have rejected your covenant, torn down your altars, and put your prophets to death with the sword. I am the only one left, and now they are trying to kill me too." (v. 10 NIV)

By speaking the truth of what he felt, Elijah was able to identify the root of his own depression. His words reveal what is known as a victim mentality. A victim mentality is a mindset that you adopt because of negative circumstances. It is throwing your hands up and saying, "I am where I am because everybody else is where they are and doing what they do." This victim mentality can show up any number of places. It can show up in racism, genderism, or classism. In adopting it, you put off being responsible for making the changes you need to make in order to better your situation. Blaming others never improves your own situation. In this case, Elijah cast blame on God. He threw everyone else under the bus and basically said he was the only one left who was worth his salt.

This mentality is what got Elijah depressed. He thought that if he was the only one left worthy of much of anything at all, then why would God allow Jezebel to chase him? Why wouldn't God have stopped the chase in order to preserve His faithful servant? Elijah didn't like God's approach and so, instead of maneuvering within the chase itself, he wanted to give up. He wanted to play the victim card.

In football, two teams battle it out head-to-head. Both teams are trying to get to opposite ends of the field. Every time one team tries to throw a pass, the other team looks for ways to intercept it. Or if one team tries to run with the ball, the other team tries to block them. If a kicker attempts to kick a field goal, the other team will try to knock the ball down so it will not reach the goal. That's just how the game is set up.

Now, what would happen if one team went out to play and the first time the other team sought to stop them, they ran over to the referee and complained that they were getting in their way? Or what if they chose to go sit down on the bench because who would want to play with such big bullies anyhow? I can tell you that if any team in the NFL adopted that mindset, they wouldn't last long. They would live in a perpetual cycle of defeat. What's worse is that their defeat would be their own fault.

Living in a victim's mentality only hurts yourself. It keeps you from learning how to block the opponent. It keeps you from discovering your own potential. It prevents you from growth. If you choose to spend all of your time focusing on how to change other people or other systems or anything you think is out to harm you, you will live in a continual state of depression. There are some things in this life that are just not going to change. Similar to football, we do face an opponent. The opponent is trying to stop our progress or make so much noise that we can't think straight. The opponent is going to try to block our attempts at touchdowns and field goals. That's just life. You can't focus your energy on trying to change someone else. That boss is not going to change. That mate may never change. Those kids might never change. The job situation may not change. Or the health situation. But if you choose to live for what you hope will change, you become the victim.

Now, please don't misunderstand me. You may be a victim. You may have been treated unfairly. It may not be right. In fact, it could even be evil that happened to you. But being a victim and living with a victim's mindset are two very different things. A victim recognizes his or her ability to get back up and keep going in spite of the reality of our situation. A person who lives with a victim's mindset does not. They blame. Accuse. Put down. Whine. Pout. Sit down. And, like Elijah, say it's everyone else's fault. Yet many of us are blocking our kingdom encounter and the supernatural move of God because we have grown too comfortable playing the role of the victim. We want a pat on the back rather than a point in the right direction.

It could be a racial issue, social issue, class issue, relational issue, or spiritual issue. But whatever it is, you are not stuck in it. Stop being stuck. Yes, Elijah was wronged. He was all alone. But God didn't stoop down and pat him on the back. No, God told Elijah to go stand on the mountain before Him. Then, when Elijah stood there, God brought a great wind and a great earthquake and also a great fire. We read,

> Then a great and powerful wind tore the mountains apart and shattered the rocks before the LORD, but the LORD was not in the wind. After the wind there was an earthquake, but the LORD was not in the earthquake. After the earthquake came a fire, but the LORD was not in the fire. (vv. 11–12 NIV)

Elijah, already despondent and crying out to God, was led by God to a place only to suffer the fate of three major disasters. First was the wind. Then came the earthquake. After which was the fire. Yet despite all of the fear and concern those three situations created in Elijah's soul, God did not choose to meet him in the midst of them. We need to remember this for our own situations in life. Because sometimes we feel that when things get really bad, God somehow owes it to us to show up and rescue us. Or, at least, He owes it to us to show up and give us some explanation. When natural disasters hit, we look to Him to be there. But in the case of Elijah, we see that this is not always how God operates.

Following the three calamities that were sure to shake Elijah to his core, we read where God did show up: "And after the fire came a gentle whisper. When Elijah heard it, he pulled his cloak over his face and went out and stood at the mouth of the cave" (v. 12–13 NIV).

Elijah heard God's whisper. He was still listening after all he had just experienced. When God had first brought Elijah to the cave, Elijah was at his lowest. Can you imagine how he felt after the three natural disasters? And yet Elijah still listened to hear God's voice. It wasn't a shout. It wasn't even God calling from the heavens. God chose to speak to Elijah in a gentle whisper. God wasn't in the wind. He wasn't in the earthquake. He wasn't in the fire. He was in the space left behind. He was in the quiet stillness of His presence.

Far too often we look for God to show up in the supernatural or extraordinary experiences of life. But most often, God will show up in the ordinary space of our time. Which is why one of the approaches of the enemy is to clutter your thinking by keeping so many thoughts going on at all times. In our busy culture, we rarely take time to pause and be still. But that is where Elijah heard from God. And it is where we can hear from Him, too.

RECEIVING THE RIGHT INFORMATION

When God did speak, He asked Elijah the same exact question as before, "Why are you here?"

You might have thought at this point Elijah would say something different from what he said before. And perhaps God was seeking to startle him to the point of saying something different from what he said before. I'm sure you know how spiritual someone can suddenly get when it looks like danger is imminent. Maybe Elijah would clean up his words and hide his real despair after going through the wind, earthquake, and fire. Maybe he really didn't want to die after all. Maybe he would beg for his life after experiencing three catastrophes that could have claimed it. Sometimes major catastrophic events can shake a person enough to make them rethink what they thought or said before it happened. But not Elijah. Elijah remained true to himself. He remained true to what he authentically felt and believed. He was stuck in a victim mentality, and that's just where he was. So when God asked him why he was there in His presence, Elijah answered the exact same way he had the first time:

> "I have been very zealous for the LORD God Almighty.
> The Israelites have rejected your covenant, torn down
> your altars, and put your prophets to death with the
> sword. I am the only one left, and now they are trying to
> kill me too." (v. 14 NIV)

Thus, when God heard Elijah's answer and saw the stubborn depth of his own self-pity, He responded by giving him an instruction on what to do next. Now, keep in mind, God didn't offer him sympathy. He didn't commiserate in the pain. No, Elijah was His prophet who had a purpose he needed to fulfill. And as is possible for all of us, he had gotten stuck in the rut of victimhood.

But God didn't scold him either. He didn't blame him. No, He did as any good parent would: He simply told him to get back up and keep going. He told him what he needed to do and how it would play out, instilling in him the confidence he needed to continue. Then He also let him know that what he had said earlier wasn't actually the truth. God gave him more information. He told Elijah that he wasn't alone after all. In fact, there were seven thousand people who had not bowed the knee to Ba'al. We read,

> The LORD said to him, "Go back the way you came, and go to the Desert of Damascus. When you get there, anoint Hazael king over Aram. Also, anoint Jehu son of Nimshi king over Israel, and anoint Elisha son of Shaphat from Abel Meholah to succeed you as prophet. Jehu will put to death any who escape the sword of Hazael, and Elisha will put to death any who escape the sword of Jehu. Yet I reserve seven thousand in Israel—all whose knees have not bowed down to Baal and whose mouths have not kissed him." (vv. 15–18 NIV)

Elijah had become so psychologically drained and spiritually worn out that he had thought he was alone. He wasn't open to God's petition. He wasn't open to being sent out on any more missions. He wanted to quit. He questioned everyone he saw. He didn't know who to trust. But in the stillness of His presence, God let him know there were seven thousand other people who shared the same faith, same commitment, same loyalty as he had. Elijah's suicidal, fear-based thoughts had been created from misinformation. He hadn't had the right information. Because of his wrong information, he had wanted to quit. But God had a calling for him. God had a petition for Elijah, and in order for him to heed it, God needed Elijah to experience Him privately first. Thus, Elijah's kingdom experience resulted in him obtaining new data that motivated him to move forward with a new petition from God. From that new information and new calling, he found his hope again. He found his confidence again. He found the strength, courage, and power to get up and continue in his calling.

Yet God not only told Elijah about the seven thousand. He also gave Elijah someone with whom he could continue in ministry. We read in the next few verses,

> So Elijah went from there and found Elisha son of
> Shaphat. . . . He took his yoke of oxen and slaughtered
> them. He burned the plowing equipment to cook the meat
> and gave it to the people, and they ate. Then he set out to
> follow Elijah and became his servant. (vv. 19, 21 NIV)

God gave Elijah someone with flesh and blood in order to serve with him in what he had been called to do. You see, sometimes your kingdom encounter will involve God sending you an angel when you are in need. Other times, God will lead you to His presence when you are despondent. And then still other times God will give you a friend who can embrace you and lift you up. In Elijah's case, he was given all three. God knew Elijah's spirit was frail and his mind had been worn down, so He gave him Elisha to help remind him of the right perspective when life got confusing or too challenging for him.

God's kingdom encounters will meet us where we are and give us exactly what we need. Yes, you may still get discouraged in this life. Life is hard. But if you will cry out to God and be authentic with what you feel and what you are thinking, He will meet you where you are and lift you out of it.

CHAPTER 9

Encountering God's Presence

The story is told of an S-4 submarine that was run into by a ship off the coast of Massachusetts. The submarine sank, and the entire crew was trapped in a prison of death. Great efforts were spent trying to rescue the crew from this sunken submarine. But all attempts failed.

One of the deep-sea divers who was part of the rescue team heard some knocking coming from inside the sub. It was Morse code. Someone was tapping Morse code against the steel wall of this submarine. When the deep-sea diver detected what was being sent to him by code, he responded very quickly. The question that had been tapped repeatedly against the steel coffin called out: Is there any hope?

Many of us today find ourselves in a similar situation. We feel trapped. We feel as if we are suffocating beneath a pile of uncertainty, doubts, and fear. Our one question remaining is a simple one but one that is not always answered in ways we can decipher. Our heart's cry rings out with all the strength we have left to muster: Is there any hope?

It is okay to acknowledge if you are in the group of those who ask this question. It is okay to wonder if there is any way out of life's seeming menagerie of hopelessness that we all find ourselves in at one point or another. You may question whether there is any solution to the constant drip, drip, drip of discouragement you face. It could seem as if one negative thing after another shows up. As soon as you pay off a debt, another one appears. As soon as you make it through a relational trial, another one crops up with someone else. As soon as you fix an item in your home or car, something else breaks. As soon as your heart gets lifted, something else seems to latch a hold of it to pull it back down. It can seem like an unforgiving cycle that never allows you to escape. And the only words left for you to voice are simple ones, but also words that carry so much weight: Is there any hope?

When you are in a hopeless situation, another one of the key questions you most likely ask—if you even dare to ask—is: Where is God? If you know God, love God, serve God, then do you ever wonder why you can't see Him working in your life or feel His presence when you need it most? God seems to be so far away at the times when we need Him to be closest. You may wonder how to get Him back if you feel like you have lost Him along the way.

Such is the situation written about in Luke 24.

This account is one of the greatest stories in the entire New Testament, yet it is one we don't hear about often. It's great because of what it says about the specific context and the insights it gives us into the happenings of that day. But it is also great because of what its truth means for you and me today.

HOPELESSNESS BLINDS

The story starts out in the most ordinary of situations. Two people are walking on their way back home. We read in verses 13–14,

> And behold, two of them were going that very day to a village named Emmaus, which was about seven miles from Jerusalem. And they were talking with each other about all these things which had taken place.

Scripture doesn't mention both names of the individuals. We are told that one of them is Cleopus. Since they were traveling to the same home, many people assume that it was Cleopus and his wife walking together. Yet verse 25 explicitly says there were two men. Whoever they were, they were walking home in the midst of a great spirit of discouragement. Their heads were down. Their stride was slow. Questions stirred in their hearts like moths looking for a place to land. No doubt, one of the questions floating around was simply this: Is there any hope?

After all, they had just seen their dreams dashed on a cross and sealed with a spear. All the good they had hoped Jesus would bring to their lives and to their nation just died with Him, nailed to a wooden beam between two thieves. Things couldn't have gotten any worse. At least not according to how they perceived them. They walked in a daze. And the reason we know that is because when Jesus approached them in His glorified body, their eyes prevented them from truly seeing Him. They had lost their spiritual sight. Depression and despair can do that to you, can't it? Things can get so bleak that you forget how to see things spiritually. You forget how to recognize God in your midst. In fact, those times when we feel so down and alone, as if God were someplace far away, are often the times when He is the closest. It's just that our own pain has prevented us from recognizing Him. We have become consumed with the chaos and uncertainty both within and around us that we have become blind to everything else.

I don't want to be too hard on the two people walking that day. I don't want to judge them for missing Jesus in their midst. They had given their whole lives to Jesus. They had devoted their time, talents, treasures, and trust to Him. And He had told them He was the Messiah. He had told them He could and would solve Israel's problems through the establishment of God's promised kingdom.

He was their Deliverer, Emancipator, and Savior. They believed Him. They bought in. They woke up each day wondering whether today was the day that good would win. But then evil kept creeping in. So much so that their world seemed flipped upside down. The King who was to set them free now hung on a tree. For these two to walk home discouraged is understandable. They were human. They viewed life through the grid they had been given. And the view was bad. Very bad.

Maybe you can relate. Disappointments come hardest after a season of serving the Lord. We would never say that we are entitled to His promises and blessings, but when we commit our time and efforts to Him and then life comes up short, it's easy to wallow in self-pity. It's easy to let your head hang. It's easy to miss God Himself when He is walking close enough to you that you feel you can literally reach out and touch Him. You are human. You view life through the grid you have been given. And sometimes that view is bad. Very bad. Hopelessness has a way of building plaque around the soul. It's hard to scrape it off when it sticks on. When hopelessness sets in, it can seem like there is no daylight around. It's easy to give up, stop going to church, and give in to your emotions, allowing them to grow into despair. It's easy to miss Jesus standing right next to you simply because you cannot see Him.

Jesus was there with these two individuals as they walked home. And He is with you as well. But what good is a Jesus you can't recognize? Not as good as a Jesus that you can. Which is why it is important to understand what prevented these two people from seeing Jesus. They had been with Him for a while by then. But why couldn't they see Him?

Jesus answers that question for us. He tells us in verse 25, "O foolish men and slow of heart to believe in all that the prophets have spoken!" Jesus says they had two problems. First, they were foolish. Second, they had lost their faith. They had stopped believing. Whenever you stop believing, you stop seeing. Anytime you stop believing, you get spiritual cataracts.

It's easy to stop believing when all hope looks gone. But

when hope vanishes, you ought to look for Jesus more than ever because He could be right beside you. You just can't see Him. When hopelessness overrides your faith, your eyes become blinded to what is really going on. Some of your greatest answers to some of your greatest problems are occurring during times of your greatest discouragement. I understand that you may not be able to see the answer right there in front of you. I understand what it's like to face difficulty after difficulty and wonder where God is. But it is in times like these that you must press through the doubt all the more in order to reignite your faith. You must never forget that it is during times of your greatest hopelessness that Jesus is nearer than He's ever been before. You just aren't seeing Him because your faith has been swallowed by fear. It is during this time of hopelessness that you are best positioned for a kingdom encounter.

REDISCOVER JESUS

Jesus gives us insight into what we must do in order to strengthen our faith in times of despair. We discover this insight in the next two verses, where it tells us what He did for the two people walking to Emmaus:

> "Was it not necessary for the Christ to suffer these things and to enter into His glory?" Then beginning with Moses and with all the prophets, He explained to them the things concerning Himself in all the Scriptures.
> (vv. 26–27)

When you lose hope and want to throw in the towel because what you thought God was doing doesn't look like it's working, two things must happen in order for you to see Jesus anew. The first thing you need to do is revisit all of Scripture. The story doesn't tell us that Jesus gave them a Bible verse and went on His way. No, He started at the beginning and explained to them the truth of what they were experiencing concerning Himself, based on Scripture. It was a seven-mile walk, and I imagine they walked at a slow pace, which gave Jesus the opportunity to go through the Scripture and show them all they needed to know about Him.

This is the key that unlocks the door to let you out of your cell of hopelessness. You must open up your Bible and look for Jesus. You may not realize this, but the story of Jesus starts in Genesis. Jesus doesn't start at the virgin birth as recorded in Matthew. Jesus shows up all throughout the Old Testament. For example, when Israel was going through the wilderness, they ran out of water. God told Moses to hit the rock. The rock then spewed out the water. But later in the New Testament, Paul explains that when the rock opened up and gave them water to drink, that Rock was Christ. We read, "And all ate the same spiritual food; and all drank the same spiritual drink, for they were drinking from a spiritual rock which followed them; and the rock was Christ" (1 Cor. 10:3–4).

The Old Testament is full of Jesus Christ. He is the master key that unlocks the truth of Scripture. As a pastor of a large church, I have a master key. This master key allows me access into any and every room on our campus. Now, certain staff have certain keys that give them entrance into certain locations and rooms. But what I was given allows me to access everything. Similarly, a lot of Christians have keys to certain sections of Scripture. They read a story here or dissect a story there, and they have gained a certain amount of understanding. But Jesus is the master key that unveils the entirety of Scripture. Far too few recognize this reality and tap into it. You must look for Christ in the Scripture even when you can't see Him right next to you. Jesus, the living Word, opened up the written Word and spoke to the two people walking on the road, weighed down by life's disappointments. The One who wrote the Truth was also the One delivering the sermon to them. He opened the Bible to them and let them see Him.

During times of hopelessness, you need a kingdom encounter with the Living Lord. The Bible is indispensable for giving you back your hope and experiencing the encounter you need most. Thus, when you can't see Jesus, you must open your Bible and pray, "Show me Jesus." You are to look for a Person, not just a doctrine. You want to see Christ revealed, not just Christ talked about. You need to exercise faith in what God says. It's okay to admit to God that you can't see Him, feel Him, hear Him, or even sense that He is there. But after you admit it, you must hunt for Him. He told you that He will never leave you nor forsake you. Take Him at His Word. The role of the Bible is to give you a kingdom encounter with the mind of God. You must approach it with a desire to exercise faith in it. You can pray, "Holy Spirit, I am opening Your Word. Show me Jesus." He is the One who unlocks the door to your future.

The Bible is like a grounding wire. It holds you steady. The Bible is foundational in giving you what you need for life. But you must approach it through the abiding of the Holy Spirit to help you see all that is to be seen. You need to pray like Paul: "I pray that the eyes of your heart may be enlightened, so that you will know what is the hope of His calling, what are the riches of the glory of His inheritance in the saints" (Eph. 1:18).

In fact, Jesus expressly anointed Paul with the ministry of opening eyes and hearts so others could see Him. We read of this when Paul shares his conversion testimony and calling with King Agrippa:

> "And when we had all fallen to the ground, I heard a voice saying to me in the Hebrew dialect, 'Saul, Saul, why are you persecuting Me? It is hard for you to kick against the goads.' And I said, 'Who are You, Lord?' And the Lord said, 'I am Jesus whom you are persecuting. But get up and stand on your feet; for this purpose I have appeared to you, to appoint you a minister and a witness not only to the things which you have seen, but also to the things in which I will appear to you; rescuing you from the Jewish people and from the Gentiles, to whom I am sending you, to open their eyes so that they may turn from darkness to light and from the dominion of Satan to God, that they may receive forgiveness of sins and an inheritance among those who have been sanctified by faith in Me.'" (Acts 26:14–18)

Jesus called him to "open" the eyes of the lost and struggling so that they would turn from darkness to light and from the kingdom of Satan to the kingdom of God. Jesus is the revelation of Truth, which is why seeing Him and hearing from Him is so critical. The two who walked on the road to Emmaus understood this. As they approached their village, Jesus acted as if He were to keep going. But they "urged Him" to stay with them for the evening. Their Bible study had led to a desire for a more personal, intimate fellowship. Their hopelessness was being lifted. Discouragement had been given a spark that flickered just enough to begin to drive doubt from their hearts. They wanted more. But they didn't just want His teaching. They wanted Him. They wanted Him to hang out with them and stay a while. When Jesus saw their sincere desire for Him, He remained with them. And as He reclined at the table to eat dinner with them, their eyes were opened. Scripture says,

> So He went in to stay with them. When He had reclined at the table with them, He took the bread and blessed it, and breaking it, He began giving it to them. Then their eyes were opened and they recognized Him. (Luke 24:29–31)

They didn't recognize Him in the Bible study. Their eyes were still closed during the seven-mile walk. It wasn't until they fellowshipped with Him that they saw who He truly was. The recognition came when He broke the bread. Why do you think they recognized Him when He broke the bread? Where do your eyes go when someone is breaking bread? Your eyes will typically go to their hands. As He lifted the bread to bless it and break it, they must have seen the nail prints in His hands. Their eyes were opened, and they saw the Lord. Bible doctrine should lead to experiencing personal intimacy with the Savior. The written Word should lead to the Living Word. It is this intimacy that makes biblical truth come to life. Without it, there is no life (John 5:39–40). This is why the ordinance of communion is so important. It uniquely connects us with the person of Christ (1 Cor. 10:16–17).

ABIDING IN CHRIST

Do you know your greatest revelation of Jesus is going to come in the midst of your most hopeless situation? Your greatest kingdom encounter will come when you are at your lowest point emotionally, spiritually, and physically. Your greatest manifestation of Christ will come when He seems the farthest away. It will not necessarily come during a small group study. Neither will it necessarily come during a church service. Your eyes will be opened to Jesus and all He is both in you and for you when you are hanging out in His presence, watching Him, and keeping your eyes focused on His every move. Had the two individuals been so preoccupied with their own situation, getting their own drinks, food, or straightening their home for a visitor, they would have missed it. They would not have seen Him lift the bread. The point is: You have to be looking.

Jesus doesn't burst out of a telephone booth, rip His shirt open, and reveal an "S" for Savior before He takes off, flying for all the world to see. He could do that if He wanted to. Rarely does He reveal Himself in obvious ways. Jesus usually reveals Himself in the ordinary moments of life, when He sees you are focusing on Him because you want to. Not because your back is up against the wall, or you need an answer right now. Not when you are pleading. No, the two individuals on the road saw Jesus for who He was when they paused to do something very typical in life: eat dinner. They had set aside their concerns for enough time to dine. And that's when they saw Jesus. When they gave up their worry, they released their fears. They chose to abide. If only for a moment. But keep in mind, it takes only a moment for you to recognize Jesus and be assured of His presence in your life.

John 15 says that if you will abide in Him and His Word, and He abides in you, you can do anything. You can overcome anything. Your prayers will be answered. Because your prayers will be aligned in Him. You are experiencing Him in an ongoing manner. Jesus doesn't want you to just learn about Him, study some stories, post some Scripture verses, and throw up some prayers. He wants a relationship with *you*. That's the kingdom encounter you need to be pursuing. The one that happens twenty-four hours a day, seven days a week. It's called *abiding*.

This abiding kingdom encounter transforms you. It lifts you. It strengthens, protects, and preserves you. It also compels you to share the truth of Jesus with others. Just like it did with the two on the road to Emmaus. The rest of the story goes on to share how Jesus' presence changed not only their outlook but also their emotions and their actions:

> They asked each other, "Were not our hearts burning
> within us while he talked with us on the road and opened
> the Scriptures to us?" They got up and returned at once
> to Jerusalem. There they found the Eleven and those with

them, assembled together and saying, "It is true! The
Lord has risen and has appeared to Simon." Then the
two told what had happened on the way, and how Jesus
was recognized by them when he broke the bread. (Luke
24:32–35 NIV)

Seeing Jesus set their hearts aflame, so much so that they
couldn't keep it to themselves. That's what any kingdom encounter with Jesus will do. It will motivate you to tell about
Him to anyone else you can. One of the reasons evangelism has
declined so sharply in our current Christian climate is that we
have so few true kingdom encounters with Christ. He has lost
preeminence in our personal lives, families, and churches—
which puts the whole culture in jeopardy. When you encounter
the living Lord and the one, true Savior—especially when all
hope is gone—you will talk about it. You will share His love,
power, and presence with others. You won't be afraid to bring
up the name Jesus. You won't care what others think or what
others say. Because anyone who loves you enough to join you in
the midst of your hopelessness and misery, and lift you out, deserves to be praised. He deserves to be celebrated. He deserves
your commitment to glorifying His name.

When God shows up for you, and you get to experience
Him up close and personal, be sure to tell others. So many people need their own encounters as well. You have been chosen
to take the message of His hope to a world in need. You are
an example from whom others can learn to experience Jesus
more fully. Boldly share what Jesus has done in your life once
you have had a kingdom encounter with Him. In doing so, you

will shine the light Paul spoke about to King Agrippa in order to release the captives from darkness. You will open the way for a movement of kingdom encounters to occur across the nation and around the world.

CHAPTER 10

Encountering God's Preeminence

When a head coach on an NFL team perceives that the referee has made a wrong call, awarding a key play to the opposition, he throws out a red flag. This red flag signals that the referee needs to review the play. Obviously, the coach believes that the referee has made a mistake.

There are times in our lives when we want to throw a red flag out on God. It looks like He has missed something and made a wrong call. It looks like He didn't know what He was doing because if He did, He wouldn't have called things that way.

In those times, we want to reach into our pocket and pull out our red flag and yell, "God, you missed this one! You blew it. Review it, because you're obviously wrong." In John 11, we get to see what happens when two sisters throw a red flag out on God and, as a result, wind up with one of the greatest kingdom encounters of all time.

DOING THE RIGHT THING, BUT . . .

In this chapter, we learn a man named Lazarus has become sick. His sisters, Martha and Mary, send word to Jesus and ask Him for His help. We read,

> Now a certain man was sick, Lazarus of Bethany, the village of Mary and her sister Martha. It was the Mary who anointed the Lord with ointment, and wiped His feet with her hair, whose brother Lazarus was sick. So the sisters sent word to Him, saying, "Lord, behold, he whom You love is sick." But when Jesus heard this, He said, "This sickness is not to end in death, but for the glory of God, so that the Son of God may be glorified by it." Now Jesus loved Martha and her sister and Lazarus. (John 11:1–5)

The first thing to note from this scenario is that Martha and Mary started out in their difficult situation by doing the right thing. They took their problem to Jesus. When they found themselves in a hopeless situation, they did what seemed best: they called out to Jesus.

We also learn from the passage that Lazarus, Martha, and Mary had a special relationship with Jesus. The sisters had said, "Lord, behold, he whom You love . . ." We're not talking about somebody who hasn't been to church in a while, or somebody who doesn't care about spiritual things. We're not talking about somebody who has no relationship with Jesus. We're talking about somebody whom Jesus loved. In verse 5, we see that Jesus didn't just love Lazarus but that He cared deeply for his two sisters as well. Jesus had shared a frequent and unique fellow-ship with all three of them.

Another thing we notice from the passage is that when the two sisters told Jesus about their problem, He gave them hope. They told Him about their struggle, and He sent back a word of expectation because He said, "This sickness is not to end in death." Martha and Mary heard comforting reassurances: "It's going to be all right. It's all fine. It's covered. It's not as bad as it seems. God is going to be glorified. Relax."

So far, so good. Lazarus gets sick. Martha and Mary send word to their close friend and miracle maker, Jesus. Jesus sends word back telling them not to worry because all is well. The problem comes, though, when Lazarus dies. After having done the right thing, and after having experienced a relationship with God and having gotten hope from His word, things not only stay bad for the two sisters but get worse. When Martha and Mary had started this pilgrimage, Lazarus was sick. Now, Lazarus is dead.

Martha and Mary experienced contradictory and volatile emotions. Lazarus is sick. Martha and Mary reach out to Jesus for help. Jesus sends back hope. Lazarus dies. Not only does he die, but Jesus then has the audacity to tell his disciples after-wards that "Lazarus is dead, and I am glad for your sakes that I was not there" (John 11:14–15). Hold up. Jesus didn't just say that, did He? It's bad enough for Jesus not to make it a priority to come to his friends in their time of need, but then to say that He's glad that He wasn't even there? If Martha and Mary got wind of Jesus' talk, they might wonder, *What? We called you. We needed you. We wanted you. We trusted You. You loved us.*

We were in pain. You had the ability to ease that pain. And You spread it around to your homeboys that You are glad that You weren't even here! Come on, Jesus, what kind of friend are You?

If that isn't enough to rip a heart in two, there's more. In an earlier verse, we read, "So when He heard that he was sick, He then stayed two days longer in the place where He was" (John 11:6). Jesus knew that Martha and Mary needed Him, and yet He delayed. In the center of their crisis, Jesus delayed. You would have thought that given the fact that He loved them, He would have gone to their aid in a hurry. But He did just the opposite. Jesus intentionally delayed responding to a disaster in the lives of three people whom He loved.

The trip He needed to take in order to reach them probably wasn't all that long. If we skip ahead to verse 18, it tells us that Bethany was only two miles away from Jerusalem. Assuming Jesus had returned to Jerusalem by the time He received news of Lazuraus, He would have been just a morning's walk away. He would have been close enough to get there in time to fix their problem, to bring calm to their chaos.

Maybe you have been in a sickening situation like Martha, Mary, and Lazarus at one point in your life. Maybe you have found yourself where you did everything that you knew to do, you called out to Jesus, but He didn't come. Maybe you are there right now. Things seem to be going from bad to worse. You love Jesus. Jesus loves you. You call out to Jesus, but He doesn't come through. If you are in a situation like that right now, I want to remind you that you are more in God's will now than you have ever been in your life.

In Lazarus's scenario, we have a desperately needed kingdom encounter situation. We have Jesus loving Lazarus and Lazarus loving Jesus. We have people praying; Martha and Mary are calling out to Jesus. We have Jesus doing nothing and hanging out in His current location while stuff is falling apart in Lazarus's location. In God's sovereignty, He chose to delay.

If you can't see God coming through for you right now even though you are doing everything you know to do, I want to challenge you not to throw in the towel just yet. Because when God delays, He always delays for a greater purpose. You might not be able to see that purpose right now because you live within the confines of linear time. But God knows what's just around the corner. And it's worth the wait.

A Right-Now God

Jesus, always capitalizing on a moment, turned His delay into a teaching time for His disciples. We read in verse 11 that Jesus says to them, "Our friend Lazarus has fallen asleep; but I go, so that I may awaken him out of sleep." In Jesus' delay, He introduces a new concept to them: Sleep. The word "sleep" is used only of believers in the New Testament when they die. So Jesus introduces a new definition to His disciples to explain a certain reality to them. Jesus wants to give His disciples a different understanding of their physical realm.

Instead of viewing death as a cessation of existence, He illustrates it as merely a transfer of consciousness, like sleep. When you are asleep, you are still very much alive. Most of us do not fear going to sleep. In fact, most of us probably look forward to going to sleep. The reason we are not afraid to go to sleep is because we know that all we are doing is transitioning into another arena of awareness. By sleeping, we are not ceasing to exist.

Jesus used the word "sleep" when talking about Lazarus's death because He wanted them to look at things differently. But the disciples responded to this new truth in the way the disciples often did: they didn't get it. We read in verse 12 that "the disciples then said to Him, 'Lord, if he has fallen asleep, he will recover.'" They were still thinking of sleep in the normal sense of the word. But the passage goes on to tell us, "Now Jesus had spoken of his death, but they thought that He was speaking of literal sleep. So Jesus then said to them plainly, 'Lazarus is dead. . . . Let us go to him'" (John 11:13–15).

Teaching time is over. The disciples didn't get it. So Jesus heads over to Martha and Mary. Jesus will see Martha and Mary at different times and in different locations, but they both greet Him by saying the exact same thing. They must have had a family discussion earlier while they were waiting because they both agreed on the same conclusion. In verse 21, we hear Martha saying, "Lord, if You had been here, my brother would not have died." And in verse 32, Mary says, "Lord, if You had been here, my brother would not have died."

The first words out of both Martha's and Mary's mouths when Jesus comes are essentially, "Jesus, this is Your fault. Because if You would have been here, we wouldn't be here. We wouldn't be dealing with sickness, death, loss, and emotional pain. The only reason we're going through this now is because You weren't here when You were supposed to be."

The unspoken question through all of their words is: What good is a God who isn't there when you need Him the most?

Now, these two sisters are very interesting personality types. We see from the story that Martha is the boisterous, out-spoken one who will confront you. Mary, on the other hand, is the quiet one. Because these two sisters are so different, when Jesus arrives on the scene of Lazarus's death, we hear the same words but witness two different deliveries. Both of the sisters are disappointed. We know that because they both say the same thing. But Martha bolts out of the door of the house, runs down the road and immediately confronts Jesus.

Martha had heard the promises of God. She had banked on the promises of God. She had gotten a great word from God, that her brother's sickness was not unto death. But all of a sudden, things went south, and all she wanted to know was, "How could You, Jesus? Where were You, Jesus? Why did You leave me in my mess without You, Jesus?"

On the other hand, Mary is so upset that she won't even leave the house. Mary stays home. Martha bolts down the road while Mary, I suppose, says, "I'm not talking to Him. If He wants to talk to me, He can come to me. Because all of this is His fault." Yes, Christians are sometimes disappointed with the Lord.

Jesus starts with Martha, and Martha wastes no time at all. Martha wants to go deep so she throws out a theological statement that is profound: "Even now I know that whatever You ask of God, God will give You" (John 11:22). It's easy to read over that statement and miss its meaning, and if you do, you've lost out on a huge spiritual truth. Martha is in a hopeless situation.

We're talking death here. It doesn't get any more hopeless than when something or someone dies. However, even though there is no hope for her situation, she says she knows something. She reaches back to what she knows to be true in spite of the circumstances she is in. She knows whatever Jesus asks His Father to do, He will do.

See, Martha has gone to Bible college, as it were. She's learned some theology because we hear it come out in her words. What she says boils down to, "Jesus, I'm disappointed with You, but I still believe what I learned in those Bible classes I took with You, and I know God will respond to You. You can ask Your Daddy to do whatever You want, and He will do it."

Jesus replies to her faith by saying, "Your brother will rise again" (John 11:23). Watch what just happened. Martha laid out a general theological truth: what You ask of the Father, the Father will do. Her general theological truth then leads her to a personal word from Jesus: "Your brother will rise again." In Jesus' affirming of her objective truth, He gives her a personal word. He said, "Your brother . . ." In other words, if you do not believe in His general revelation with regard to what He says in His Word in providing principles and precepts, He's not going to give you specific application. But because Martha affirmed general revelation, He gave her specific application. Then, if we peek ahead at verse 25, we will see that when she wanted clarification on the application that came from the revelation, Jesus Christ gave her Himself. He revealed, "I am. . . ."

The great problem we often find in our churches today is that you can come to church and get revelation without leaving the church and having personal application. This happens because you do not believe the revelation through the preached Word. You just heard it, clapped about it, nodded with it, or said "Amen" to it. But unless you affirm and receive it, you will never get specific application, like Martha did. In order to hear the "secret" things of God that are personal with our names on it, we must first believe and act on the general revelation that He has given. Abraham, sacrifice your son. Moses, remove your shoes. Disciples, cross the sea.

When Martha gets this personal word that her brother will rise again, it then launches her even deeper into a theological discussion. We read in verse 24, "Martha said to Him, 'I know that he will rise again in the resurrection on the last day.'"

Jesus then answers by throwing in a zinger. He says, "I am the resurrection and the life; he who believes in Me will live even if he dies, and everyone who lives and believes in Me will never die" (John 11:25–26). Jesus says that until, and unless, you turn your theology about Me into an experience with Me, it will remain doctrine on paper and not a reality in your existence. Martha had the right theology. Martha said, "I know he will rise again." Jesus responded, "I am the resurrection and the life."

Martha spoke in the future tense. Jesus spoke in the present tense. Martha said, "He will." Jesus said, "I am." It's all about the tense.

She is saying her theology tells her that he will rise again in the last day. But Jesus is saying while that is true of the future, He is also a right-now God. He's not just a tomorrow God. He is a right-now God in the middle of a dead situation. Jesus wants

Martha to know that not only will He be the resurrection in the sweet by and by, but He is also a resurrecting God in the nasty here and now.

Once He makes that clear, Jesus tags on a question. He asks her, "Do you believe this?" Jesus wants to know if she not only believes her theology, which is correct, but also believes that He is who He says He is right now. Not just for the future in anticipation, but for now. Does she believe His personal revelation?

That's a question that He asks us, too. Because it's easy to have a good theology for tomorrow, and a bad theology for today. You can believe all of the theological truth that you were taught but not experience its relevancy in your life right now. God doesn't just want a relationship with us where we can spout theology. He wants a relationship with us where we've seen theology come alive in our kingdom encounters with Him. He wants the truth about God to become an "I am" reality. That's what He was saying to Martha.

If God lets something or someone die, it's so we can see what God can do in a dead situation. Because only God can bring death back to life.

IF YOU BELIEVE

After Jesus spends time talking with Martha and Mary and has compassion for the emotional state they are in, we read what He does next:

> So Jesus, again being deeply moved within, came to the tomb. Now it was a cave, and a stone was lying against it.

Jesus said, "Remove the stone." Martha, the sister of the deceased, said to Him, "Lord, by this time there will be a stench, for he has been dead four days." (John 11:38–39)

Jesus made a simple request, "Remove the stone." Martha, on the other hand, goes into a discussion of mortuary sciences. Jesus says, "Remove the stone." Martha essentially says, "Wait, I think we need to talk about this first."

Let's start by taking a look at what Jesus did not say. Jesus did not ask for an autopsy report. He did not request an analysis of the situation. He did not ask for information about which He was already completely aware. Regardless, Martha interrupts to let Jesus know that what He is asking isn't practical. She lets Jesus know that what He is asking isn't logical. She brings up the fact that what He is asking them to do makes no biological sense.

"Let me explain, Jesus," Martha basically says. "In case You don't know how this works, I will tell You. See, my brother has been dead for four days now. Do You remember that delay that You did, Jesus? Okay, good, because I remember it, too. With that delay, Lazarus has been dead for four days. When someone has been dead for four days, Jesus, rigor mortis sets in. This leads to bodily decay. The worms have begun eating him. So, just in case You need a little more information, that means there is going to be a stench. My brother is in a stinky situation. If You would have been here, he wouldn't be in this situation. But now that You are here, I don't think removing the stone is our best option."

What Martha didn't know was that when God wants to give you a kingdom encounter, He will often make a request that makes absolutely no sense. He will make a request that is illogical. Lazarus is literally behind a stone. Jesus asked Martha to remove the stone and doesn't give them any more information than that.

When God is getting ready to do something significant in your life that involves a deliverance from a situation gone bad, or a resurrection of a situation that has died, it will often include an illogical request. This request given to Martha makes no practical sense.

Jesus' instruction to her was pretty simple: "Remove the stone." He wasn't asking her to do rocket science. He just said, "Remove the stone."

A multitude of scenarios in the Bible displaying God's divine intervention and kingdom encounters came with a request that didn't make sense. Once you add human logic to the Word of God, you attempt to cancel the effect of the Word of God in your situation. The moment God says one thing, and you say, "Wait, but, I think . . ." you have just attempted to cancel what God has said.

Jesus doesn't want to have a discussion about the stone He has told us to remove. He doesn't want to know how big the stone is. He doesn't want to know how long the stone has been there. He doesn't even want to know how dead the dead is behind the stone. All Jesus wants you to do is remove the stone.

After Martha's argument, it sounds like Jesus is getting evangelically annoyed. He replies, "Did I not say to you that if you believe, you will see the glory of God?" (John 11:40).

Jesus sounds like a parent here, "Did I not say? Didn't you hear what I said? Weren't you listening? Were you not paying attention? I said remove the stone, and you want to have a discussion about the aspects of death? You want to talk about how bodies rot? You want to get into this long discussion and inform the omniscient One who already knows all things? Did I not say?"

A lot of us, like Martha, are delaying our deliverance by discussion and intellectual human logic. We're spending so much time discussing how illogical the expectations of God are that we can't get around to deliverance. So we find our situation stuck in a grave.

Jesus said, "Did I not say?" He is reminding Martha about their conversation they had just had. He's reminding her of the theological discussion that had already taken place. They didn't need to have another one. Remember, we read it earlier,

> "I am the resurrection and the life; he who believes in Me will live even if he dies, and everyone who lives and believes in Me will never die. Do you believe this?" (vv. 25–26)

Martha had gotten very spiritual during that interchange. She had said, "Sure, Jesus, I believe it. I trust You. You're the wheel in the middle of a wheel. You're the Rose of Sharon, and the Balm of Gilead. You're all that, and more. I believe, Jesus!"

"Okay, then," said Jesus. "Remove the stone."

"Wait," said Martha, "let's talk."

The problem is that Martha went no further than theology. Martha went no further than the biblical truth she had learned had never needed to apply. She went no further than the theological information that was good for a classroom, good for a teaching session, and good for notes in her notebook, but she never had needed to use at a deep level in her life.

Martha is a lot like us, and we are a lot like Martha. We believe in a Jesus we can talk about, but not a Jesus we know well personally. We believe in a God who works in the Bible; He just doesn't work today. We believe that He can reverse things for others; He just can't do it for me.

Jesus said, "Did I not say?" He said it as plainly as He could. "'Did I not say to you that if you believe, you will see the glory of God?'" This is another one of those nuggets we find in the Bible. Don't misread that verse. Jesus doesn't say if you see, you will believe. He says that if you believe, you will see.

Here's the principle: To experience the living Christ in your dead situation, belief must precede sight because without faith it is impossible to please God. Faith precedes sight. Belief requires no empirical evidence to validate what you are doing. There is nothing to taste, smell, touch, hear, or see in order for you to believe. There is nothing the five senses can grab because if there is, then it is no longer faith. You don't have to see something to know it's real. But what you do have to do is act in faith based on the integrity of God's Word.

God says, "The just shall live by faith" (Rom. 1:17 KJV; see also Hab. 2:4). So how do you know when you have faith? First, I'll tell you how you don't know. You don't know you have faith by how you feel. You don't know you have faith because you feel faith-ish. You only know you have faith when you remove the stone; when you do the thing God has asked you to do. If you're not doing the something He told you to do, then you're not having faith. If you're discussing it, you're not at the point of faith yet; you're at the point of discussion. If you're thinking about it, you're not at the point of faith yet; you're at the point of mere thought.

You are not at the point of faith until God sees that stone move. Faith is expressed in your feet. Not just in your feelings.

What can you expect to happen when you move the stone? Jesus told Martha that if she will believe, she will see the "glory of God." The glory of God is seeing God manifest Himself in your kingdom encounter.

But it's important, also, to note what Jesus did not say Martha would see. While Jesus does tell Martha that something is going to happen, He does not give her the details of what that something will be.

That's important to realize because here's what a lot of us do. We go to God and say, "God, tell me what You are going to do behind the stone when I move it so that I can decide if it's worth me moving the stone. Give me the details, God, and then I'll exercise my faith."

But what we need to remember is another deep, but simple, theological principle: If God doesn't get us to respond to His revealed will—to remove the stone—we will never get to see His secret will. You will never know what He's going to do behind the stone until you move the stone. As long as you keep discussing the stone, it will always be a secret. God says, "Remove the stone, then I'll show you what I'm going to do in secret behind the stone."

But Martha had told Jesus, "If I remove the stone, it's going to stink." Martha's statement can apply to many of us because many of us are in a stinky situation. It's smelly. Things have been rotting there for a while. So what do we do? We come up with meetings to discuss moving the stone. We meet too much. We meet too long. A lot of these meetings need to be only one meeting. Because all we're going to discuss in the second or third meeting is the same stone.

We're discussing that maybe we should put the stone on one end and scoot it out just a bit first. Or we're discussing how many people will be needed to move the stone. We're discussing how some of us just don't feel like moving the stone in the morning. Some of us would prefer to move it at night. Or some of us think we should wait until December, for that matter. Ten years pass, and we're still discussing moving the same stone a million different ways. While we're having our meetings year after year, guess what's happening behind the stone? Stuff is getting stinkier. Stuff is rotting.

And Jesus is still standing there saying, "Didn't I tell you? Remove the stone. You're making this too difficult. You're making this too deep."

"But Jesus," we say, "what are You going to do when we remove the stone?"

"None of your business," He replies. "Because I'm not going to tell you My secrets until I see your faith. I see your faith when you remove the stone."

Verse 41 tells us that they finally got it. "So they removed the stone," without any more discussion. The next word in the passage is critical. It says, "Then . . ." After they did what Jesus told them to do, Jesus did His thing. Jesus did not do His thing until after they had removed the stone.

We read, "Then Jesus raised His eyes, and said, 'Father, I thank You that You have heard Me. I knew that You always hear Me; but because of the people standing around I said it, so that they may believe that You sent Me'" (John 11:41–42). Notice that Jesus and His heavenly Father had already discussed the matter ("You have heard Me"). But only the exercise of faith would bring the answer into historical reality.

A great truth in the Bible comes from the book of Hebrews and shows up in the verse we just read. Hebrews speaks of Jesus when it says, "Therefore He is able also to save forever those who draw near to God through Him, since He always lives to make intercession for them" (7:25). To intercede for somebody is to be a go-between. A lawyer in a courtroom is an intercessor for the client. Jesus is our go-between with God the Father (1 John 2:2).

The Bible declares that Jesus is seated at the right hand of the Father, ever making intercession. For most of us, that is a theological concept that is meaningless and ethereal. But if you can grasp that truth and apply it to your relationship with God, it can change everything. Because if you will remove the stone, simply do the thing Jesus has revealed to you to do—and you can discover what that is by abiding in Christ and letting His words reach deep within you—then Jesus will talk to God for you.

Abide in Him. Discover what God's viewpoint is on the matter. Learn what He is asking you to do through His Word. Then do it; remove the stone. Remove it, like Martha and Mary did. They removed the stone.

Then Jesus prayed. God responded. We read, "When He had said these things, He cried out with a loud voice, 'Lazarus, come forth'" (v. 43). Jesus called forth a specific person in a specific situation in response to specific faith exercised by specific people. Guess what those specific people got? They got a resurrection.

They got a miracle. They got a kingdom encounter.

Lazarus was trapped in a grave, and only God could get him out.

YOUR I AM GOD

Have you ever been trapped in a grave? You've tried being part of the *Night of the Living Dead*. You've tried to walk out of the tomb on your own, but it just keeps dragging you back. You are trapped. Stuck. If this describes your situation, you need more than resuscitation. You need more than deliverance. You need a resurrection. Do you remember what Jesus said to a dead situation? He said, "Come forth."

God wants to make some dead scenarios come forth. He wants to make some dead futures live again. He wants to make some dead careers come alive once more. He wants to make some dead marriages resurrected. He just can't get husbands and wives to remove the stone. They want to keep talking about all of this other stuff when God says, "All you need to do is remove the stone. Just do the thing that I told you to do, and then I will call forth life."

Martha and Mary didn't make life come forth. All they did was remove the stone at His word. Then Jesus created a miracle.

Someone reading this book needs a miracle. You need a resurrection. That means there has been a death. Something in your life has died, and you need God to call it back to life.

Someone is trapped in an addiction. You've tried everything you know to get out of it, but it doesn't seem to work. What you need is a resurrection. Someone is trapped in a poor self-image. You've tried what the counselors and self-help books and television programs have told you to do, but you are still trapped. What you need is a resurrection. It could be that you need your financial situation to be resurrected, or a relationship in your family, an attitude, your health, or hope to come alive again.

Whatever it is, God can take your dead or dying scenario and call forth a resurrection. He can take what looks like a rotting situation and give it new life. He's just waiting for you to remove the stone. We want to keep talking about it. We want to discuss it. We want to understand it. All Jesus wants is for us to do it. When we do what God says to do in faith, God is free to bring forth life.

That's good news. In fact, that's great news. I want you to take courage in the news that Jesus is the I AM God. He is the Right-Now God for your trial and test. As dead as it may look doesn't mean that's as dead as it has to be. As hopeless as it may appear doesn't mean that's as hopeless as it really is. It just may mean that God is waiting for you to remove the stone. Ask Him if you don't know what stone He wants you to remove. Tell Him you are willing to do it if He will reveal to you through His Word what He wants you to do.

Martha removed the stone. Jesus called Lazarus by name. Lazarus, who was once dead, got up again.

God wants to be the same all-powerful I AM God for you. God wants to give you more than theology. He wants to give

KINGDOM ENCOUNTERS

you a kingdom encounter with Himself. He wants to be real to you. Having a medical book is nice. Having a doctor is better. Having a law book is nice. Having a lawyer is better. Having a menu is nice. Having a meal is better.

What Jesus is saying in John chapter 11 is that He is a God who wants to give you a taste for yourself that He is the I AM God. Reading about Him is good. Hearing about Him is good. But if you leave this life without having deeply experienced God Himself, then you may have known a nice truth from a distance, but you will never have known all He can do for you. You will never know what it is like to hear the God who created the universe call your scenario by name. You will never know the power in hearing Him say, "Career, come forth. Marriage, come forth. Health, come forth. Relationship, come forth. Hope, come forth. Future, come forth. Family, come forth. Finances, come forth. Gratitude, come forth. Peace, come forth. Significance, come forth."

Whatever is dead or dying in your life can be called forth. Jesus can call even dead things back to life. And the excellent part about that is when He does, you won't need somebody else to tell you how good God is because you will have experienced Him for yourself. You won't need somebody else to tell you how great God can be because you will have seen Him for yourself.

God longs to be more than just theology on a shelf. He wants to be real to you right now. To accomplish this, sometimes He allows us to get, or even puts us, in seemingly hopeless situations. He lets something die for the express purpose of letting us experience a resurrection. Because God knows that when we see Him for who He really is, we will never see life the same again. It is in making Jesus preeminent in the midst of our crisis that will bring the experience of God into clear focus.

God wants us to take this new sight and view all of life differently, even the ordinary experiences that we face. He wants us to view them through spiritual eyes rather than through the eyes of a physical world that defines our existence day by day. The reason we're not experiencing more resurrections is because we are too earthbound. We are too tied to the physical definitions and expectations of life that we miss the spiritual.

Because we are too earthbound, we don't remove the stone. Because we don't remove the stone, we don't get our resurrections. But today, if you are tired of your grave, sick of your cemetery or claustrophobic in your casket, all it takes is for you to remove the stone. Ask the Holy Spirit to reveal to you from God's Word what He wants you to do. Discover God's viewpoint on the trial you are facing. Tell Him that you will do it even though you don't like it, don't understand it, or it doesn't make sense. Do it anyway, in faith. Then, watch your faith be made sight.

Faith is acting like something is so even when it is not so in order that it will be so simply because God said so.

It's time for a kingdom encounter. It's time for your resurrection.

The Urban Alternative

The **Urban Alternative (TUA)** equips, empowers, and unites Christians to impact *individuals, families, churches,* and *communities* through a thoroughly kingdom agenda worldview. In teaching truth, we seek to transform lives.

The core cause of the problems we face in our personal lives, homes, churches, and societies is a spiritual one; therefore, the only way to address it is spiritually. We've tried a political, social, economic and even a religious agenda.

It's time for a **kingdom agenda**.

The kingdom agenda can be defined as the visible manifestation of the comprehensive rule of God over every area of life.

The unifying central theme throughout the Bible is the glory of God and the advancement of His kingdom. The conjoining thread from Genesis to Revelation—from beginning to end—

is focused on one thing: God's glory through advancing God's kingdom.

When you do not recognize that theme, the Bible becomes disconnected stories that are great for inspiration but seem to be unrelated in purpose and direction. Understanding the role of the kingdom in Scripture increases the relevancy of this several-thousand-year-old text to your day-to-day living, because the kingdom is not only then; it is now.

The absence of the kingdom's influence in our personal lives, family lives, churches, and communities has led to a deterioration in our world of immense proportions:

- People live segmented, compartmentalized lives because they lack God's kingdom worldview.
- Families disintegrate because they exist for their own satisfaction rather than for the kingdom.
- Churches are limited in the scope of their impact because they fail to comprehend that the goal of the church is not the church itself, but the kingdom.
- Communities have nowhere to turn to find real solutions for real people who have real problems because the church has become divided, in-grown, and unable to transform the cultural landscape in any relevant way.

The kingdom agenda offers us a way to see and live life with a solid hope by optimizing the solutions of heaven. When God is no longer the final and authoritative standard under which all else falls, order and hope leaves with Him. But the reverse of that is true as well: as long as you have God, you have hope. If

God is still in the picture, and as long as His agenda is still on the table, it's not over.

Even if relationships collapse, God will sustain you. Even if finances dwindle, God will keep you. Even if dreams die, God will revive you. As long as God and His rule are still the overarching standard in your life, family, church, and community, there is always hope.

Our world needs the King's agenda. Our churches need the King's agenda. Our families need the King's agenda.

In many major cities, there is a loop that drivers can take when they want to get somewhere on the other side of the city but don't necessarily want to head straight through downtown. This loop will take you close enough to the city so that you can see its towering buildings and skyline, but not close enough to actually experience it.

This is precisely what we, as a culture, have done with God. We have put Him on the "loop" of our personal, family, church, and community lives. He's close enough to be at hand should we need Him in an emergency, but far enough away that He can't be the center of who we are.

We want God on the "loop," not the King of the Bible who comes downtown into the very heart of our ways. Leaving God on the "loop" brings about dire consequences as we have seen in our own lives and with others. But when we make God, and His rule, the centerpiece of all we think, do, or say, it is then that we will experience Him in the way He longs for us to experience Him.

He wants us to be kingdom people with kingdom minds set

on fulfilling His kingdom's purposes. He wants us to pray, as Jesus did, "Not My will, but Yours be done" (Luke 22:42). Because His is the kingdom, the power, and the glory.

There is only one God, and we are not Him. As King and Creator, God calls the shots. It is only when we align ourselves underneath His comprehensive hand that we will access His full power and authority in all spheres of life: personal, familial, ecclesiastical, and societal.

As we learn how to govern ourselves under God, we then transform the institutions of family, church, and society using a biblically based kingdom worldview.

Under Him, we touch heaven and change earth.

To achieve our goal, we use a variety of strategies, approaches, and resources for reaching and equipping as many people as possible.

BROADCAST MEDIA

Millions of individuals experience *The Alternative with Dr. Tony Evans* through the daily radio broadcast playing on nearly **1,400 Radio outlets** and in over **130 countries**. The broadcast can also be seen on several television networks and is available online at tonyevans.org. You can also listen or view the daily broadcast by downloading the Tony Evans app for free in the App Store. Over 20,000,000 message downloads/streams occur each year.

LEADERSHIP TRAINING

The Tony Evans Training Center (TETC) facilitates educational programming that embodies the ministry philosophy of Dr. Tony Evans as expressed through the kingdom agenda. The training courses focus on leadership development and discipleship in the following five tracks:

- Bible and Theology
- Personal Growth
- Family and Relationships
- Church Health and Leadership Development
- Society and Community Impact Strategies

The TETC program includes courses for both local and online students. Furthermore, TETC programming includes course work for nonstudent attendees. Pastors, Christian leaders, and Christian laity, both local and at a distance, can seek out The Kingdom Agenda Certificate for personal, spiritual, and professional development. For more information, visit: tonyevanstraining.org

The Kingdom Agenda Pastors (KAP) provides a *viable network* for *like-minded pastors* who embrace the kingdom agenda philosophy. Pastors have the opportunity to go deeper with Dr. Tony Evans as they are given greater biblical knowledge, practical applications, and resources to impact individuals, families, churches, and communities. KAP welcomes *senior and associate pastors* of all churches. KAP also offers an annual summit held each year in Dallas with intensive seminars, workshops, and resources.

Pastors' Wives Ministry, founded by Dr. Lois Evans, provides *counsel, encouragement,* and *spiritual resources* for pastors' wives as they serve with their husbands in the ministry. A primary focus of the ministry is the KAP Summit that offers senior pastors' wives a safe place to *reflect, renew,* and *relax* along with training in personal development, spiritual growth, and care for their emotional and physical well-being.

COMMUNITY & CULTURAL INFLUENCE

National Church Adopt-a-School Initiative (NCAASI) prepares churches across the country to impact communities by using *public schools as the primary vehicle for effecting positive social change* in urban youth and families. Leaders of churches, school districts, faith-based organizations, and other nonprofit organizations are equipped with the knowledge and tools to *forge partnerships* and build *strong social service delivery systems.* This training is based on the comprehensive church-based community impact strategy conducted by Oak Cliff Bible Fellowship. It addresses such areas as economic development, education, housing, health revitalization, family renewal, and racial reconciliation. We assist churches in tailoring the model to meet specific needs of their communities while simultaneously addressing the spiritual and moral frame of reference. Training events are held annually in the Dallas area at Oak Cliff Bible Fellowship.

Athlete's Impact (AI) exists as an outreach both into and through the sports arena. Coaches can be the most influential factor in young people's lives, even ahead of their parents. With the growing rise of fatherlessness in our culture, more young people are looking to their coaches for guidance, character development, practical needs, and hope. After coaches on the influencer scale fall athletes. Athletes (whether professional or amateur) influence younger athletes and kids within their spheres of impact. Knowing this, we have made it our aim to equip and train coaches and athletes on how to live out and utilize their God-given roles for the benefit of the kingdom. We aim to do this through our iCoach App as well as resources such as *The Playbook: A Life Strategy Guide for Athletes.*

Tony Evans Films ushers in positive life change through compelling video-shorts, animation, and feature-length films. We seek to build kingdom disciples through the power of story. We use a variety of platforms for viewer consumption and have over 50,000,000 digital views. We also merge video-shorts and film with relevant Bible study materials to bring people to the saving knowledge of Jesus Christ and to strengthen the body of Christ worldwide. Tony Evans Films released its first feature-length film, *Kingdom Men Rising*, in April 2019 in over 800 theaters nationwide, in partnership with LifeWay Films. The second release, *Journey With Jesus*, in partnership with RightNow Media, is scheduled to release in spring 2021.

RESOURCE DEVELOPMENT

We are fostering lifelong learning partnerships with the people we serve by providing a variety of published materials. Dr. Evans has published more than 100 unique titles based on over 50 years of preaching whether that is in booklet, book, or Bible study format. He also holds the honor of writing and publishing the first full-Bible commentary and study Bible by an African American, released in 2019. This Bible sits in permanent display as a historic release in the Museum of the Bible in Washington, DC.

For more information, and a complimentary copy of Dr. Evans's devotional newsletter, call (800) 800-3222 *or* write TUA at PO Box 4000, Dallas, TX 75208, *or* visit us online at:

www.tonyevans.org

Acknowledgments

I want to thank my friends at Moody Publishers for their long-standing partnership in bringing my thoughts, study, and words to print. I particularly want to thank Greg Thornton for his friendship over the years, as well as his pursuit of excellence in all he does for Moody Publishers and Moody Radio. I also want to publicly thank Duane Sherman, Kevin Emmert, Gabe Smith, and Connor Sterchi for their help in the editorial process. In addition, my appreciation goes out to Heather Hair for her skills and insights in collaboration on this manuscript.

COMPLETE THE KINGDOM TRILOGY

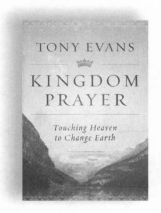

There is much God won't do in a Christian's life apart from prayer. In this practical overview, Tony Evans covers a variety of topics about prayer, including its principles, power, and purposes. He will help you see prayer's critical importance and encourage you to make it a dominant mark of your life.

978-0-8024-1484-7

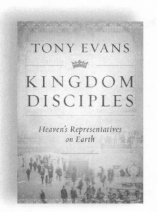

In *Kingdom Disciples*, Tony Evans outlines a simple, actionable definition of discipleship to help the church fulfill its calling. Readers will learn what a disciple is and cares about, how to be and make disciples, and what impact true discipleship has on the community and world.

978-0-8024-1203-4

also available as eBooks

MOODY
Publishers®
From the Word to Life®

MORE FROM TONY EVANS
THE KINGDOM PASTOR'S LIBRARY

978-0-8024-1831-9   978-0-8024-1830-2   978-0-8024-1833-3   978-0-8024-1832-6

The Kingdom Pastor's Library is a series that brings you a concise, complete pastoral philosophy and training from Tony Evans.

Faithful. Powerful. Practical. Become a Kingdom Pastor today.

also available as eBooks and audiobooks

MOODY
Publishers®

From the Word to Life®